To Jan
my sweet friend
from WYP. Have fun
with this book!

Rosalie Irwin Hayzol

Pasta e
Fagioli

Array of Italian Meats

Rosalie Fiorino Harpole

ROSALIE
SERVING
ITALIAN

Photographs by David Schultz

Creative Director - Paul Povolni

Copyright © 2007 by Rosalie Fiorino Harpole

All rights reserved

Published by Rosalie Fiorino Harpole

58 Madden, Troy, MO 63379

Printed by:

Publication Print Group

St. Louis, MO

Manufactured in the United States of America

ISBN-13: 978-1-4242-1638-3

Library of Congress Cataloging in Publication Data

www.rosalieservingitalian.com

rosalie@rosalieservingitalian.com

4

Contents

DEDICATION

- This, my first cookbook, is written for the glory of God. As in every thing I do or ever hope to accomplish, I give Him the praise.

- To my beloved husband Bill, who says he's 100 pounds Italian gained from all the taste testing he did to help me get these recipes just right.

- To my three children Scott, Jeff, and Dana, who have been my greatest supports for anything my heart has set out to accomplish.

- To my loving daughters-in-law, Jennifer, and Tami, who are like my own daughters, and to my son-in-law, David, who is a great husband for my daughter, Dana.

- To the most beautiful grandchildren in the world: Taylor Ryan Harpole, Ross David Harpole, Grant Nehemiah Carleton Harpole, Max Geoffrey Harpole, Roman Anthony Harpole, Reagan Brack Harpole, Alexandra Von Harpole, Elijah Harpole Schultz and the newest baby, Nicholas Fiorino Harpole.

Acknowledgements

The inspiration to write a cookbook was birthed in my heart while supervising the daily meals at the Old Threshers Country Fair in a small town called Elsberry, Missouri. It was the last day of the fair, and we had served about 2,500 meals in just three days. A dear lady came up to me and said, "We have so enjoyed these meals. Would you consider writing them down, so that you will always be with us?" It was not the first time that I had been asked that question, or other questions like "When will you ever open your own restaurant?" Up until then I had always been content to cater Italian food for both small and large events, and do the benefit dinners for my church family and community. I always enjoy teaching cooking classes to the students in our Christian/community school, or occasionally writing an Italian recipe for our local newspaper. When I got home from the fair, the lady's words kept speaking to my heart. I thought of my family, whom I have enjoyed serving all of my life, and the many friends that I have been privileged to meet from all over the world. And, yes, doesn't everyone want to leave a part of themselves to the ones they love? So the work took flight, and I soon found out that you just don't write a cookbook by yourself.

I must acknowledge all the great celebrated Italian cooks and chefs who helped me with Italian history, customs, and traditions. Authors like, Lidia Matticchio Bastianich, who wrote *Lidia's Italian -American Kitchen*, Jeff Smith's, *The Frugal Gourmet Cooks Italian*, Mark Bittman's, *How to Cook Everything*, and Giada De Laurentiis's *Everyday Italian*, opened up a whole new Italian world for me. I grew up cooking many of the same dishes, and had a general idea where some of them came from, but, the history and culture behind them were enlightening. To them, I say thank you. I will make a trip to Italy because of your inspiration.

Thanks to the nurses and doctors at Lincoln County Medical Center, where I work as a registered nurse, for all the recipes you helped taste test and critique. Thank you, family members who helped me remember recipes that I may have forgotten. Thanks to my son-in-law, David Schultz, for the fantastic food photos, and for his photographic talent all through the book. Appreciation is given to Guillermo Gomez owner of St. Louis Color Photography, for the cover picture. Tami Harpole, thanks for your family photos and a few others and to Debbie Slaughter for the charity photos. Thanks to Paul Povolni for artistic design and layout and to my sweet husband, Bill Harpole for hours and hours of editing. Also, thanks to Christine Frank, the final editor, Judy Peckham my printer-broker, and Publication Printing Company, St. Louis, Missouri. Most of all, thank you Lord, for leading me every step of the way.

INTRODUCTION

I am the daughter of Italian immigrants. My father's family was from northern Rome, and my mother's family was from Sicily. Together, my mother and father had three children, Josephine Ann, William Louis and me, Rosalie Rita. I learned to cook at a very early age. My mother always helped her friend, "Miss Mary the cook", as we called her, cater the Italian weddings. As my mother's cooking knowledge increased, so did ours. I can remember how happy she was to learn how to make brozzaloni, a big stuffed rolled steak, putting it in the Sunday pasta sauce. This continued for many years, until she eventually catered Italian food on her own. Since my mother loved to entertain and have company over, she was constantly creating her own Italian dishes. She also loved to cook the tried and true classics, such as her homemade ravioli. My father grew Italian herbs, so we always had fresh basil, cilantro, rosemary and many others. During the Christmas holidays, my mother would make hundreds of Italian cookies, wrap them in small trays, and pass them out in the community. She was also known for her warm Italian bread, which my father would bring to town on Saturdays and sell. When the Lord took my mother home at the age of 76, there was not only a void in our family, but also in the community. She died in the month of September, and when it got closer to Christmas, many of the business people in our town began to say how much they would miss Ann Fiorino's Italian cookies.

It was at this point in my life that I realized that if the Italian traditions in my family were to stay alive, it was up to me. That year, 1982, during the first week in December, I gathered every Italian cookie recipe that my mother had and was able to make 4,000 cookies. I made trays for every family in our church and many of the business people in our town. Everyone was so surprised that they immediately asked, "Are you going to take the place of your wonderful mother? Without hesitation, I said 'of course." From that day to this, the Lord has helped me to continue with the Italian customs that were important to us in our family, especially serving the wonderful Italian meals that I grew up with. Being blessed to be the wife of a minister, there was always someone dropping in, many of them traveling missionaries, or evangelists and their wives, or sometimes just church families or friends. It was fun to be able to serve them Italian classics, such as *Red Sauce with Penne Pasta*, or *Shrimp Fettuccini*. Not only was it fun, but the memories will last forever.

When asked the question, "Why do you want to write a cookbook"? I had to stop and think. Was it just to write down a bunch of recipes? Immediately, I knew it was so much more. The main purpose of this book is **to portray with every recipe, the importance of preserving family relationships.** It is not about making a meal and consuming it, but about being able to sit down with your family altogether and bond in love. I know in the busy day that we live, it is sometimes very difficult to gather together for meals. But let me encourage you to do so. When our children grow up what stories will they have to tell? Do they even know their relatives? Maybe we should all evaluate what is more important in life. Is it about so many out-of-the-home activities that constantly keep us running, or a sit-down meal with our family, and some quiet time to enjoy one another? My purpose in writing this cookbook is for you to sit at my table and enjoy *Pasta con Broccoli,* to think of me, and have fun. Your purpose is to serve *Pasta con Broccoli* to your family, so that they can bond with you, and think of you years from now with a warm memory. Whether you are a family of four, or a single mom or dad, this book is for you and yours.

I want to say also that I could not have entertained so many without the help of my children. To reward them, many times I would get out my best china and set the table only for them. They could ask for any dish or dessert and together we would thank God for His many blessings. May God bless you my friend, and please, keep **Serving Italian.**

William and Ann Fiorino

Endorsements

"Somewhere back before the advent of the fast-food chain and the one minute meal, families came together around the kitchen table to share of themselves with one another. It was their forum for all conversation, modeling and growth. Such was the case in our home wherein food was more about our philosophy of life than the mere sustenance it brought. Every recipe represented a way of living and it spoke to who we were and what we would become. The greatest lessons were taught to us in the kitchen; the stove was our mother's pulpit and we were her faithful congregation. As you read through these many pages you will find recipes for both life and dinner, but maybe they are the same."

Jeffrey C. Harpole

"We live in a fast-food age. Our families are pulled in many directions; soccer, after school jobs and evening classes are some of the things that pull us away from one another. But my mom was different than most; she chose to set aside the dinner table as a gathering place for our family. While the pretence was feeding her family dinner, we all knew it was really an evening show.

Sometimes, the show was generated by our family. One of my favorites was the continual question asked of my brother Jeffrey. Could he take Dad up on his standing offer of five dollars, if he could stand still for three minutes? (Jeff was never able to collect those elusive five dollars.) At other times the show would come to us from outside our family unit. My mom's cooking tended to lend itself to people readily accepting an invitation to eat with us on a regular basis.

We would rub elbows at the table with people who, after finishing an extraordinary plate of pasta, would jump up from their seats and (I am not making this up) run around the living room in some sort of celebratory victory lap. You can understand why, if as a child one of my brothers or I slept through a meal for whatever reason, we would be very upset.

The watermark for excellent food and entertaining dinner companions has been set quite high by my mother. If you use the power of this cookbook wisely perhaps one day you too will see celebratory victory laps in your living room."

Dana Beth (Harpole) Schultz

*(**Endorsements** . . . continued on page 12)*

*(**Endorsements** . . . continued from page 11)*

"I have lived by a simple rule. If you want a real meal of whatever ethnic culinary taste your appetite calls for, find the original creators. They know how to fix it because it was born in them and their offspring will carry on the family tradition.

We were always happy to accept an invitation from Pastor Harpole to speak at the church in Troy, Missouri, and for more than one reason. They are a great family and their children are so marvelous to be around, talented, and so courteous. But the highlight of every special week-end of services was the smell and the taste of genuine Italian cooking. If Rosalie Fiorino Harpole ever had the idea of opening a 'Trattoria' she would have become wealthy. Her Italian dishes are simply wonderful. Having lived in Italy for some time and eaten in homes and cafes and tasted just about everything Italians can serve up, I speak from experience that it's not all palatable, but at the Harpole home everything is 'molto bene'. Rosalie Fiorino Harpole, thank you for those great meals and the warm Italian welcome always extended when we were with you.

I would encourage every reader if you cook at all, try some of these fine Italian dishes. You'll be hooked."

Mervyn D. Miller,
Former missionary to Italy
Foreign Missions Division
United Pentecostal Church Int.

From Rosalie's Kitchen to Yours

Preparing and serving your special Italian dish is not only gratifying but can be a lot of fun. However, one thing that can cause great stress and unravel you is discovering that you are missing a key ingredient that the recipe is requesting. If you are going to serve Italian, your kitchen must be well equipped. When you get this cookbook you will be able to say, "Tonight we're serving Italian straight from Rosalie's kitchen to ours." Let me make the following suggestions for the basic Italian stocked pantry.

- **Olive Oil:** Extra virgin and full-bodied mild olive oils are my favorites. For some dishes, I find the extra virgin too strong. So I always have good mild olive oil on hand. I recommend the Bertolli Classico brand for both the extra and mild olive oils.

- **Fresh Garlic:** There is just no other substitute! Look for the pods that have a little pink or purple tinge, this usually means they are fresh. Some cloves are bigger than others, so use your judgment when making your recipe. Don't be afraid to use it and always have it on hand.

- **Coarse Garlic Salt with Parsley:** Use this to sprinkle chicken, fish, pork, and beef before preparing your recipe. You will love the flavor it renders. I recommend Lawry's Coarse Garlic Salt with parsley.

- **Fresh Herbs:** If at all possible, grow an herb garden. Use them fresh in the summer and dry them for the winter. If you keep dried herbs in the pantry, be sure to replace them about every six months for the best flavor. These are my favorite herbs: basil, parsley, [both curly and flat-leaf], peppermint, rosemary, dried crushed red pepper flakes, dried herbs de Provence, and of course, for our wonderful meatballs and sausage, fennel seed.

- **Vinegars:** Red wine, cider, and balsamic are some of my favorites. For good tasting sweet vinegar, try sweet Balsamic of Modena. You can mix it equal part-to-part, using a good olive oil.

- **Cheeses:** A must for the Italian kitchen! Some cheeses you will constantly use are: Parmesan, Pecorino Romano, mozzarella, and fresh buffalo mozzarella. Others that are good, but you may not use so often, are Fontina and feta. Get a cheese grater and a fresh block of Romano and oh my, what a garnish!

- **Pastas:** Always have on hand an assortment of dried pastas: angel hair, penne, fettuccini, linguine, rigatoni, and spaghetti, both thick and thin. Don't forget the soup pastas, like acini de pepe, ditali, and small shells. Get a good brand of pastas; I like Barilla.

ROSALIE FIORINO HARPOLE

- **Chicken and Beef Stock:** Used to flavor sauces, stews, and soups. If you have the time, homemade stocks are great. But if not, I recommend a low-sodium soup stock, such as Swanson. Keep several cans on hand. You will need them.

- **Marinara Sauce:** Make my homemade recipe found on page 127. It makes up quickly, and can always be frozen for later use. You will use this item over and over. If you are rushed for time, have a few ready-made jars in the pantry. I recommend the Barilla brand.

- **Salt and Pepper Garnish:** Always keep coarse sea salt or kosher salt. You will constantly use this. Coarse ground black pepper is a must to top pasta dishes and many other items. I recommend Tone's Restaurant Black Coarse Pepper. Also, keep a pepper grinder for making freshly ground coarse black pepper.

Antipasta and Appetizers

Antipasti and Appetizers

Antipasti is the first course; it means "before the meal." I can remember my uncle Joe Campise taking a fresh hot loaf of Italian bread, cutting it in half, slathering it with olive oil and cheese, and placing anchovies on both halves. He would then put the halves together, smash it down a little, and break off pieces for every one at the table while my aunt Irene was preparing the meal. This is true Italian hospitality. The guests were never to leave and say they did not have enough to eat. From before the meal, while we were talking, laughing, and enjoying the good bread, until after the meal, with a biscotti and coffee, we could honestly say we had been lavished with good food and fellowship.

Today, antipasti and appetizers have gained much popularity; with anything from *Shrimp Scampi* and *Italian Stuffed Mushrooms*, to imported Italian cheeses and prosciutto wrapped vegetables. As a child, I really didn't know what the term antipasti meant. My mother always had a bowl of *Marinated Olive Salad*, *Caponata*, green onions, and fresh bread. Maybe a fresh slice of Romano cheese, or whatever we had on hand to put on the table before the main meal. The antipasti and appetizers were just as much enjoyed as the courses to follow.

Tips about Antipasti: Almost anything can be used as an appetizer if cut into small enough pieces or served in small bowls. Whether you have light or heavy appetizers depends on the main course itself. Sometimes, just a big bowl of fresh grapes with Italian cheeses, salamis, and Italian toasted rounds is plenty. Serving *Garlic Butter Bruschetta*, *Fried Ravioli*, and *Italian Breaded Eggplant* will make a meal in itself. Be careful because appetites may be filled before you can serve your lovely meal. Of course, if time is not a problem and you have all night, serve what you will and have fun.

Polpette
(ITALIAN BREAD PATTIES)

NOTE: *My mother would make these little patties often and use them in marinara sauce over angel hair pasta. They are great as appetizers, plain or dipped in sauce.*

1 cup plain bread crumbs
1/3 cup Parmesan grated cheese
2 cloves garlic, chopped
¼ cup fresh Italian flat-leaf parsley, chopped
1 teaspoon salt
¼ teaspoon ground black pepper

6 eggs, beaten
olive oil for frying

Marinara Sauce recipe (optional) found on page 127

1. Mix together the bread crumbs, cheese, garlic, parsley, and salt and pepper. Add the beaten eggs to make a batter. Drop by heaping tablespoons into hot oil, and flatten gently to make small patties. Fry about 2 minutes, turning from side to side, until golden brown. Patties will puff up and should be airy and light. Best when served hot. Makes about 12 patties.

Marinated Olive Salad

Marinated Olive Salad

NOTE: Olives, hard salami, and Fontina cheese can be found in Italian grocery stores, or in deli departments in fine stores. This is a wonderful antipasti full of Italian flavor.

½ pound large green pitted Spanish olives
1 (12-ounce) jar Kalamata olives, drained
¾ cup celery hearts, ½" slices, strings removed
½ cup Genoa chunk hard salami, ½" small cubed
½ cup Fontina block cheese, small cubed
½ cup pepperoncini peppers, stems removed
1 teaspoon minced garlic, or more for taste
½ teaspoon dried oregano
1 teaspoon coarse sea salt
¼ teaspoon cracked black pepper, or more if desired
¼ teaspoon dried crushed red pepper flakes

¼ cup extra virgin olive oil
2 teaspoons red wine or cider vinegar

1. Mix all the ingredients together and place in large jar or covered container. Shake container to coat the olives with the seasonings. Keep refrigerated for one or two days, then remove to large bowl and let come to room temperature. Serve with warm Italian bread if desired.

Marinated Roasted Peppers

NOTE: *Roasting peppers brings out the natural sweetness, and marinating them makes them quite delicious. They are good served alone or can be used as toppings on most anything.*

3 red bell peppers

2 yellow bell peppers

1 cup olive oil

1 large clove garlic, minced

⅛ teaspoon crushed red pepper flakes, optional

1 teaspoon coarse sea salt, or more to taste

1. Preheat broiler. Place the peppers on lightly oiled baking sheet on the upper rack in oven. Broil the peppers, turning them occasionally, until all sides are evenly blackened and charred, about 20 minutes. Remove the peppers and place them in a large bowl. Cover tightly with plastic wrap to steam and loosen the skins. Let stand until cool enough to handle, and then remove from bowl.

2. Cut the peppers in half, removing the seeds and stem. With sharp knife, gently peel off the skins. Cut the peppers in strips and place in large bowl. Add the olive oil, garlic, crushed red pepper flakes, if using, and salt. Stir together. Cover and refrigerate overnight for the flavors to blend. Bring to room temperature and serve. Use as appetizers on bruschetta bread or topping on sandwiches.

Italian Breaded Eggplant

NOTE: *Enjoy these crisp eggplants as is or use them over linguine pasta with marinara or meat sauce. These eggplant crisps are so good, you will eat them like candy. Short on time? Skip the soaking. They will still be delicious.*

1 large eggplant, unpeeled
3 teaspoons salt for soaking eggplant

2 cups Progresso Italian Style bread crumbs
⅔ cup grated Parmesan cheese
¼ cup fresh Italian flat-leaf parsley
3 cloves garlic, minced
3 eggs, beaten

olive oil for frying
salt to sprinkle
Marinara Sauce recipe (for dipping), found on page 127

1. Slice eggplant thin, about ¼" thick. Let soak submerged in cool salted water for about 20 minutes. Rinse eggplant, drain, and pat dry.

2. Combine the Italian bread crumbs, grated cheese, parsley, and garlic. Mix well. Dip eggplant slices in beaten egg and then in bread crumbs.

3. Fry in hot oil on each side, about 2 to 3 minutes, being careful not to burn. Lightly salt slices while frying. The slices should be fork- tender and crisp. Add more oil as needed to complete frying. If crumbs begin to burn in bottom of pan before completing the entire eggplant, clean pan, and start a new batch. Drain fried eggplant on paper towel and transfer to platter.

4. Dip eggplant in your favorite marinara sauce. Makes about 12 to 15 slices, depending on the size of eggplant.

Italian Stuffed Mushrooms

NOTE: *Before you say no to the artichokes, just try putting them in a few of the caps. You really won't be able to tell, and they add a wonderful flavor. Make up a double batch because everyone will want seconds and thirds. These are so awesome!*

1 pound large button mushrooms (white), about 30
½ cup Progresso Italian Style bread crumbs
⅓ cup freshly grated Pecorino Romano cheese
2 tablespoons fresh Italian flat-leaf parsley, chopped
1 large clove garlic, minced
¼ teaspoon coarse sea salt
¼ teaspoon coarse ground black pepper

3 tablespoon olive oil
⅓ cup fresh crab meat,
  or imitation, chopped fine
3 marinated artichokes hearts, chopped
1 to 2 teaspoons olive oil for oiling baking pan

1. Preheat oven to 400°F. Clean mushrooms and trim off hard core bottom of stem. Remove stem and gently clean out cavity, being careful to keep cap intact. Chop a few of the soft stems (not all) and place in bowl with bread crumbs, cheese, parsley, garlic, and salt and pepper.

2. Mix and add the olive oil, crab meat, and artichokes. Stir together. Mixture should be moistened, but not "wet."

3. Stuff each cap with mixture to a little overflowing, and place stuffed-side up on lightly oiled baking pan. Bake about 15 minutes, until mushrooms are tender and stuffing is toasted on top. Serve hot for best taste. Makes 30 servings.

Stuffed
Mushrooms
with
Fried Cauliflower
and
Breaded Ravioli

Caponata
(Marinated Eggplant Compote)

NOTE: *This classic Sicilian vegetable dish can be used in so many ways. As an appetizer, to accompany meat or fish entrees, or just over your favorite sandwich, it is delicious. Keeps well in the refigerator; use it hot or cold.*

1 large eggplant, unpeeled and small cubed

3 teaspoons salt for soaking eggplant

½ cup olive oil, divided

1 medium onion, about 1 cup, small quartered

⅔ cup celery, ½" slices, with leaves

1 large red bell pepper, cored, seeded, cut into 1" cubes

1 small zucchini, cubed, about 1 cup

1 large clove garlic, chopped

1 teaspoon coarse sea salt

¼ teaspoon ground black pepper

1 (15-once) can diced tomatoes, with juice

¼ cup stuffed olives with pimento, halved

2 tablespoons golden raisins

¼ cup fresh basil leaves
    or ½ teaspoon dried basil

¼ cup cider vinegar

2 tablespoons sugar

1 tablespoon capers, drained and rinsed

1. Cut end off eggplant, and slice into ½" circles. Soak eggplant in cool salted water with heavy bowl over top to keep eggplant submerged for about 30 minutes.

2. Meanwhile, prepare the onion, celery, red bell pepper, zucchini, and garlic. Place in a large saucepan, sprinkle with the salt and pepper, and add ¼ cup olive oil. Sauté altogether for 10 minutes. Vegetables will appear translucent.

3. Rinse and drain the eggplant and cut in ½" cubes. In separate sauce pan, add ¼ cup olive oil and sauté the eggplant for 10 minutes. Combine the eggplant and the vegetables in the largest saucepan. Add the tomatoes, olives, raisins, and basil. Simmer together for 15 minutes.

4. In small saucepan, place the vinegar, sugar, and capers. Cook together about 1 minute until mixture becomes syrupy. Add to the eggplant mixture and cook for another 5 minutes. Season with more salt or pepper if desired. Makes about 4 cups.

Italian Breaded Cauliflower

NOTE: *These breaded cauliflower florets are wonderful as an appetizer, but can also be used as a vegetable side dish. If you need more bread crumbs, just make up another batch.*

1 large head cauliflower, stems removed and broken into small florets
1 to 2 teaspoons salt, added to boiling water
3 eggs, beaten

1 cup Progresso Italian Style bread crumbs
⅓ cup grated Parmesan cheese
2 cloves garlic, chopped
2 tablespoons fresh Italian flat-leaf parsley, chopped
1 teaspoon salt
¼ teaspoon ground black pepper

½ cup olive oil for frying, or more if needed
salt and pepper
Parmesan cheese for garnish

1. Cook cauliflower florets in salted boiling water just until tender, 6 to 8 minutes. Drain and set aside. Beat eggs in large bowl and add the cauliflower florets, mixing gently to coat.

2. Mix the bread crumbs, cheese, garlic, parsley, and salt and pepper together. Place in large shallow bowl. With slotted spoon, lift 2 to 3 florets out of egg mixture and into bread crumbs. Roll in crumbs until well coated.

3. Pour olive oil in large saucepan and over medium heat, fry the florets until golden brown. Sprinkle salt and pepper over florets while frying. Transfer florets to paper towel, then to large platter. Continue until all the florets are coated and fried. If oil in saucepan becomes too dark and filled with burnt crumbs, clean pan, and add new olive oil. Continue to complete frying.

4. Sprinkle cheese over cauliflower while still warm. Serve as is or dip into your favorite Marinara Sauce. Serves 6.

Appetizers:

RAVIOLI
STUFFED MUSHROOMS
BREADED CAULIFLOWER

(Time: 20 Minutes)

Fried Ravioli

NOTE: *Serve as an appetizer with* **Italian Breaded Cauliflower** *recipe, found on page 25 and* **Italian Stuffed Mushrooms** *recipe found on page 22. These ravioli are delicious, with or without the sauce.*

½ pound frozen beef or cheese ravioli

1 tablespoon salt

3 beaten eggs

⅔ cup plain bread crumbs

⅔ cup grated Parmesan cheese

2 cloves garlic, chopped

¼ cup fresh Italian flat-leaf parsley, chopped

½ teaspoon salt

¼ teaspoon ground black pepper

½ cup olive oil, or more if needed

Marinara Sauce recipe found on page 127, or sauce of your choice

1. Boil 4 quarts water, with 1 tablespoon salt added. Add the ravioli and boil until the ravioli are tender. Drain gently. Beat the eggs in large bowl, and add about half the ravioli to the egg mixture at a time.

2. In shallow bowl, mix the bread crumbs, cheese, garlic, parsley, and salt and pepper. With a slotted spoon, lift the ravioli one at a time out of the egg mixture, and coat well in the bread crumbs. Continue until all are breaded.

3. In large saucepan, heat olive oil until hot. Add several coated ravioli to the hot olive oil and fry until golden brown on both sides, 2 to 3 minutes. Remove to paper towel to drain.

4. Transfer to large platter with bowl of marinara sauce in the middle for dipping. Serve hot. This will make a large platter.

Garlic Butter Bruschetta
(WITH TOMATO AND PESTO MUSHROOMS)

NOTE: *These toasted bread slices are crunchy and wonderful. They actually melt in your mouth, and the variety will have your taste buds hopping. I'm sure you will make these over and over. The mozzarella slices are plain with just pesto for those who do not like tomatoes or mushrooms.*

1 loaf Italian crusty bread

1 stick butter, softened to room temperature

2 cloves garlic, minced

½ teaspoon coarse garlic salt with dried parsley

3 slices provolone cheese, fresh sliced from the deli

3 slices mozzarella cheese, fresh or regular

3 slices Fontina cheese

1 large round garden tomato sliced into 3 slices, 1/4" thick

½ cup homemade or Bertolli Basil Pesto Sauce

grated Parmesan cheese for garnish

½ cup mushrooms, thick sliced

1 tablespoon butter

coarse sea salt

coarse ground black pepper

grated Parmesan cheese for garnish

extra virgin olive oil

1. Preheat oven to 500°F. Cut Italian bread into nine ½" slices, cutting both ends off loaf to discard or use elsewhere. If middle slices are too large, cut in half. Place softened butter in bowl and add minced garlic and coarse garlic salt. Whisk together until smooth and butter the bread slices liberally.

2. Top 3 slices with the provolone cheese, 3 with the mozzarella cheese, and 3 with the Fontina cheese. Trim cheese to fit bread.

3. Next, working with the first 3, place a tomato slice over the provolone cheese, and place a tablespoon of the pesto sauce over the tomato. Garnish with cheese, and place slices on large cookie sheet. Set aside.

4. On the mozzarella slices, place 1 tablespoon of the pesto sauce, garnished with a little Parmesan cheese. Transfer to cookie sheet with other bruschetta.

5. Sauté mushrooms in butter until golden, 3 to 4 minutes. Place the mushrooms, divided, on the 3 slices with the Fontina Cheese. Sprinkle a little coarse salt and pepper on mushrooms to taste. Garnish with grated Parmesan cheese. Set on cookie sheet.

6. Bake in hot oven 4 to 5 minutes, until toasted. Drizzle olive oil over mushroom bruschetta, if desired. These slices can be eaten whole or cut into halves or thirds. Transfer to party tray, pierced with party toothpicks. Makes 9, 18, or 27 appetizers.

Calamari Fritti
(FRIED SQUID)

NOTE: *This is the ever popular calamari served as a well known appetizer in many Italian restaurants. Squid may be purchased at Italian meat markets.*

3 pounds squid, cleaned

1 cup flour
1 tablespoon Parmesan cheese
½ teaspoon salt
½ teaspoon coarse garlic salt with parsley
½ teaspoon lemon zest
1 cup or more olive oil for frying

grated Parmesan cheese for garnish

1. Cut squid in ½" rings. Combine flour, cheese, salt, garlic salt, and lemon zest in a shallow bowl. Dip squid rings in flour mixture to coat. Pour olive oil in a large saucepan. Deep fry the rings in hot oil 4 to 6 minutes. Remove with slotted spoon and drain on paper towel. Transfer to large platter. Sprinkle while still hot with Parmesan cheese. Serve with your favorite marinara sauce. Serves 6 to 8.

Stuffed Cherry Peppers

NOTE: *These little red and green stuffed peppers are not only attractive, but very tasty. They can also be used in salads or on your favorite sandwich.*

1 (16-once) jar Mezzetta pickled sweet cherry peppers
2 slices provolone cheese, finely chopped
2 slices prosciutto, thinly sliced, or 2 slices Genoa salami, finely chopped

1. Drain peppers. Using sharp knife, cut carefully around stem and remove. With a tiny spoon, scoop out the seeds. Mix the chopped provolone and prosciutto or salami together. Fill each cavity of the peppers to slightly overflowing. Place on tray with other appetizers for an attractive look. Makes 12.

O*live Oil Popcorn*

NOTE: *Once you've had olive oil-popped corn, it will be hard to go back to microwave popcorn, especially with the addition of the hydrogenated oils that are so bad for our health. Make a couple batches and keep on hand in sealed gallon bags, ready for when you take the kids to the zoo. Absolutely delicious!*

1 (3-quart) heavy pot with lid
3 tablespoons olive oil
½ cup Orville Redenbacher's® popping corn
salt to your taste

1. Pour the olive oil and popcorn into a heavy 3-quart pot. Cover with lid and over medium heat pop the corn, shaking the pan from side to side occasionally. When kernels stop popping, remove lid carefully. Transfer to large bowl. Add desired amount of salt and serve. Makes 10 cups.

Frittatas (EGGS) and Breakfast

Breakfast in Italian homes can be as simple as a cup of espresso coffee and a biscotti, or as in my home growing up, large and filling. Many times we had Italian sausage, fried potatoes and onions, and a mound of scrambled eggs. Because my father was a butcher, we always had a good portion of meat. He always made the Italian sausage and we especially enjoyed having it for breakfast. Frittatas are much like omelets that resemble a quiche without a crust. They are cooked slowly and undisturbed in a skillet and then baked, or put under the broiler for a few minutes to complete. My mother loved these frittatas, only she would "flip" the pan when the eggs and potatoes were half done, and then cook them on the other side. This dish was not only used for breakfast, but for meals on a week-night. I hope you enjoy the frittata recipes in this section. They are very simple to make: no flipping and all quite delicious. Feel free to create your own, like adding some pre-fried Italian sausage to the *Frittata with Potatoes and Onions* or adding chopped mushrooms to the *Frittata with Asparagus*. Since oven heat can vary, more or less time may be needed for baking the frittata.

My mother also loved pancakes and would make them often, especially on Saturday mornings, calling all three of my children from next door to join her. The recipe *Nutella Pancakes* with *Sugar Glazed Pecans* is one that I created in memory of her.

TIPS: Breakfast can be a fun time to gather the family together. Unfortunately, this is not always possible. But if you have a Saturday or Sunday open, by all means try some of these wonderful dishes. On those other days, get a loaf of Italian sliced bread, toast it up with butter and cinnamon sugar on top, and let the kids eat it on the way to school. They will love you forever!

Frittata
Asparagus

Frittata Asparagus

NOTE: *Many Italians serve frittatas as main courses as well as for breakfast. This is only one of many varieties. Since oven heat varies, more or less time may be needed for completing the frittata.*

1 tablespoon olive oil
1 tablespoon butter

½ pound asparagus, trimmed and chopped into I" pieces
1 clove garlic chopped fine
¼ cup green onion, chopped with tops (optional)
½ teaspoon salt
¼ teaspoon ground black pepper
1 large fresh tomato, peeled if desired, cored and chopped
4 to 5 fresh basil leaves, chopped

6 eggs, beaten
2 tablespoon half-and-half
¼ cup grated Parmesan or Pecorino Romano cheese

grated Parmesan cheese to garnish
parsley sprigs to garnish
coarse sea salt
coarse ground black pepper.

1. Preheat oven to 350°F. Put oil and butter in 10" oven-proof skillet.

2. Sauté the asparagus, garlic, and green onion over medium heat 5 to 6 minutes, until asparagus is crisp-tender. Salt and pepper the asparagus. Add the fresh chopped tomato and basil leaves. Cook 1 more minute.

3. Beat the eggs with half-and-half until fluffy and fold in the cheese. Pour the egg mixture over asparagus. Cook undisturbed over medium heat, about 2 minutes, until eggs begin to set and bubble, but are still runny on top. Put skillet in oven for 8 to 10 minutes. Remove skillet and transfer frittata to large round plate. The frittata should slide out of pan easily.

4. Garnish with additional cheese, parsley sprigs, and salt and pepper. Let the frittata set about 2 minutes. Cut into pie slices. Serves 4 to 6.

Basic Italian Frittata

NOTE: *The basic Italian frittata is simple, but can be almost anything you can imagine. Add vegetables, such as sautéed spinach, mushrooms, tomatoes, onions, or garlic. Add meat, such as chopped prosciutto, minced hard salami, and Italian sausage. Fresh herbs are also great, such as basil, parsley, and oregano.*

1 tablespoon olive oil
1 tablespoon butter

6 eggs, beaten
2 tablespoons half-and-half
¼ cup grated Parmesan cheese
½ teaspoon salt
¼ teaspoon ground black pepper

freshly grated Parmesan cheese to garnish
parsley sprigs to garnish

1. Preheat oven to 350°F. Put oil and butter in 10" oven-proof skillet over medium heat until warm and blended.

2. Beat the eggs with half-and-half until fluffy and fold in the cheese. Salt and pepper the eggs. Pour eggs into skillet and cook undisturbed for about 2 minutes, until eggs begin to set and bubble, but are still runny on top. Put skillet in oven for 5 to 7 minutes. Remove skillet and transfer frittata to a large round plate. The frittata should slide out of pan easily.

3. Let the frittata set 2 minutes. Cut into pie slices. Garnish with grated Parmesan and parsley. Serves 4 to 6.

Frittata
(WITH SPINACH AND PROSCIUTTO)

NOTE: *A wonderful light breakfast or main course dish. For variation, use 1 cup sliced zucchini in place of spinach or try ½ cup sliced mushrooms. Add both to the sautéed process.*

1 tablespoon olive oli
1 tablespoon butter

2 tablespoons chopped onion
1 clove garlic, chopped
3 strips prosciutto, chopped
1 cup fresh spinach leaves,
  or ½ cup frozen chopped spinach, drained
½ teaspoon salt
¼ teaspoon freshly ground black pepper

6 eggs, beaten
2 tablespoons half-and-half
¼ cup grated Parmesan cheese

grated Parmesan cheese for garnish
coarse sea salt
freshly ground coarse black pepper

1. Preheat oven to 350°F. Put oil and butter in medium 10" inch oven-proof skillet.

2. Sauté onion, garlic, and prosciutto together about 5 minutes, until onion is translucent and pro-sciutto is crisp. Add the spinach and cook together 1 to 2 minutes, until spinach is soft. Add salt and pepper.

3. Beat the eggs with half-and-half until fluffy and fold in the cheese. Pour the eggs over spinach mixture and cook undisturbed about 2 minutes, until eggs begin to set and bubble, but are still runny on top. Put skillet in oven for 6 to 8 minutes. Remove skillet and transfer frittata to a large round plate. The frittata should slide out of pan easily.

4. Garnish with additional cheese, sea salt, and ground black pepper. Let the frittata set 2 min-utes. Cut into pie slices. Serves 4 to 6.

Nutella Pancakes
(WITH SUGAR GLAZED PECANS)

NOTE: *Nutella is an Italian chocolate-hazelnut spread that is great on Italian toast or bagels. Since these pancakes are the best I have ever come across, I decided to pair them together. Now add the Sugar Glazed Pecans recipe and you have a breakfast fit for the king's castle. A little more work than a mix, but definitely worth it.*

1⅔ cup buttermilk
1 teaspoon baking soda
3 egg yolks, beaten
¼ cup melted butter
1 teaspoon vanilla

1½ cup all-purpose flour
1 teaspoon baking powder
½ teaspoon salt
1 teaspoon sugar
3 egg whites

olive oil for frying pancakes
Sugar Glazed Pecans recipe found on page 223
1 jar Nutella, chocolate-hazelnut spread

1. Put buttermilk in a 2-cup bowl and add the baking soda, mixing with a fork to dissolve. Let stand for about 5 minutes. Beat the egg yolks until fluffy and add the butter and vanilla. Add the buttermilk mixture to the egg yolk mixture and whisk together well.

2. Mix the flour, baking powder, salt, and sugar in a large bowl. Slowly add the wet ingredients to the dry ingredients, mixing together until both are incorporated and smooth. Beat the egg whites until stiff and fold into the batter. Let batter stand 5 minutes.

3. Turn heat to medium-high. In lightly oiled saucepan pour in ¼ cup batter. Fry on one side until bubbles appear on surface, then turn and fry on the other side until golden brown. Serve 3 pancakes on a plate, topped with a dollop of Nutella (heat Nutella in microwave about 5 seconds to smooth consistency) and sugar glazed pecans. If syrup is desired, try a light maple. Makes about 12 large pancakes or 24 small pancakes.

Nutella Pancakes

Frittata
(WITH POTATOES AND ONIONS)

NOTE: *My mother used to serve this frittata often as a main course, with Italian toasted bread and fresh sliced tomatoes. This is a very filling dish.*

2 tablespoons olive oil
1 tablespoon butter

1 large potato, unpeeled and sliced thin, about ⅛"
  or 4 small new potatoes, unpeeled and sliced thin
1 small onion, chopped, about ½ cup
1 clove garlic, chopped
½ teaspoon salt
¼ teaspoon ground black pepper

6 eggs, beaten
2 tablespoons half-and-half
¼ cup Pecorino Romano cheese
½ cup shredded mozzarella cheese
1 tablespoon fresh parsley, chopped
3 to 4 fresh basil leaves, shredded (optional)

freshly grated Parmesan cheese to garnish
parsley sprigs to garnish
coarse sea salt
freshly ground coarse black pepper

1. Preheat oven to 350°F. Put oil and butter in 10" oven-proof skillet.

2. Sauté the potatoes, onion, and garlic. Sprinkle with salt and pepper. Fry together over medium heat until potatoes are tender, 8 to 10 minutes.

3. Beat the eggs with half-and-half until fluffy. Fold in the cheeses and parsley. Pour the egg mixture over potatoes and cook undisturbed over medium heat about 2 minutes, until eggs begin to set and bubble, but are still runny on top. Add the basil leaves on top, if desired. Place skillet in oven for 8 to 10 minutes. Remove skillet and transfer frittata to a large round plate. The frittata should easily slide out of pan. Garnish with additional cheese, parsley sprigs, and salt and pepper. Let the frittata set about 2 minutes. Cut into pie slices. Serves 6.

Soups and Salads

Soups: Italians love soup, so much that many times soups are the main course of the meal. Grouped together with hot Italian bread and a small salad, they can be very filling. Soup broths are also added to sauces for flavor. I have included *Homemade Chicken and Beef Stock* for this purpose, which is always wonderful. But I also realize many working men and women do not have time. I recommend using a low-sodium canned chicken or beef broth for your flavoring, which have proved to be very good. Some of my fondest memories at the Italian table were enjoying a hot bowl of *Italian Beef Soup with Meatballs* or the *Italian Lentil Soup with Italian Meat and Sausage.* My mother always had a hot loaf of the Italian homemade bread, and of course we always dipped the bread into our soup. If she fixed a salad with the meal, we needed nothing else for a heavenly memory.

Tips: If you are using a small amount of pasta or quick-cooking pasta, add it directly to the soup at the end of cooking, as you will find in the *Wedding Soup* recipe. However, if you are using a large amount, or longer-cooking pasta, boil it first, but only for half the cooking time. Then add to soup and complete cooking.

Salads: Italian salads are not only delicious, but are also beautiful made up with various greens, olives, tomatoes, and pepperoncinis. The key to great salads is usually four things: The freshness of greens, a good olive oil, good tasting vinegars, and a great garnish.

Fresh Greens: Be creative and try all sorts of fresh greens such as arugula, radicchio, escarole, red, and green leafy lettuce, or tender spinach, to name a few.

Olive Oil: Use extra virgin for a rich strong taste or a full-bodied mild, which is not as strong but has a delightful flavor. I recommend Bertolli Classico brand for both. Salad dressings can be made ahead and kept in a cool place, or right on the spot using your own creativity. Be sure to try the *Salmon Spinach Salad, Insalata Caprese Salad*, and of course the *Italian Green Bean Salad.*

Pasta e Fagioli

Pasta e Fagioli
(PASTA AND BEAN SOUP)

NOTE: *Pasta e Fagioli is a delicious classic Italian soup, or as some prefer, pasta dish. It makes a lovely appearance in white pasta bowls and can easily be doubled for a larger crowd. A variation would be to use Italian sausage instead of hamburger. The soup will be a little spicier and very good. Use more or less seasonings to your taste. Enjoy!*

⅓ cup olive oil

1 medium onion, chopped

2 cloves garlic, chopped

½ cup celery, chopped

⅓ cup carrots, peeled and chopped thin

1 pound lean ground beef, crumbled

coarse garlic salt with dried parsley

⅛ teaspoon crushed red pepper, or more for your taste

¼ cup fresh Italian flat-leaf parsley, chopped

½ cup homemade or low-sodium canned chicken broth

coarse ground black pepper

coarse sea salt

1 (28-once) can whole tomatoes, hard stems removed and chopped

1 can cannellini beans, partially drained

1 cup red kidney beans

1 teaspoon oregano, or more for your taste

1 teaspoon salt

¼ teaspoon ground black pepper

½ cup ditali pasta noodles

preserved pasta water if too thick

freshly grated Parmesan cheese

1. In large saucepan, pour in olive oil and sauté onion, garlic, celery, and carrots for 15 minutes. Add the ground beef and sprinkle with the garlic salt. Continue to cook with the vegetables another 8 to 10 minutes, until the meat is no longer pink. Add the tomatoes, with juice included to the vegetable mixture. Add the cannellini beans, red kidney beans, oregano, salt, pepper, crushed red pepper, parsley, and chicken broth. Cook together another 15 minutes. Taste for seasonings and add coarse ground black pepper and coarse sea salt to your taste.

2. Boil the ditali pasta in salted water for 3 to 4 minutes. Drain and add the undercooked pasta directly to the soup. Continue to cook together 5 minutes longer. Serve in pasta bowls, garnished with plenty of Parmesan cheese and Italian bread for dipping. Serves 4.

Homemade Beef Stock

NOTE: *Homemade stocks are great in sauces and as a base to make soups. This stock may taste a little weak, but remember you will be adding seasonings to the recipe you are using. Season after you add the stock as you may need more. Another option available is the use of a good brand of low-sodium canned beef broth.*

1 tablespoon olive oil
4 pounds meaty beef bones, shank, or short ribs
1 large onion, peeled and quartered
4 celery stalks with leaves, cut in thirds
2 cups carrots, peeled, chopped coarsely
salt and pepper

4 quarts water, divided
8 to 10 fresh sprigs curly parsley
1 bay leaf
2 teaspoons salt
10 peppercorns

1. Preheat oven to 400°F. Coat large roasting pan with olive oil and in it place beef bones, onions, celery, and carrots. Sprinkle lightly with salt and pepper. Roast, turning once or twice for 1 hour or more, until all is browned.

2. Remove bones and vegetables and place in a 8-quart stockpot. Place 2 cups water in roasting pan and place over burner. Bring to a boil, scraping bits from off bottom of pan. Add to stock-pot along with 3½ quarts water. Water should just cover beef bones and vegetables. (Add a little more water, if necessary.) Add the fresh parsley, bay leaf, salt, and peppercorns. Bring water to boil and skim any foam that rises to the top. Cook about 2 hours and 30 minutes, until meat falls from bones and bones separate from one another.

3. Strain, pressing the vegetables and meat to extract as much juice as possible and discard. Cool, place in containers in refrigerator overnight. Soup should be congealed the next day. Skim hardened fat off top of soup and discard. Store in heavy 1-quart freezer bags, 1 to 2 cups in each. This broth is great in **Italian Beef Soup with Meatballs** recipe found on pages 50 and 51, or in your favorite roasts that need stock. Makes about 10 cups.

Homemade Chicken Stock

NOTE: *Homemade chicken stock adds great flavor to many of the Italian dishes we enjoy and is so easy to make. It will go a long way, kept in the freezer. If you run out, use a good brand of low-sodium canned chicken stock.*

4 pounds chicken pieces, such as leg quarters, wings, backs (no breasts)
4 stalks celery, with leaves, cut into 3" pieces
3 to 4 carrots, peeled, cut into 3" pieces
1 pound onion, peeled and quartered
2 cloves garlic, smashed, and left whole
salt and pepper

3 to 4 quarts water
8 to 10 sprigs fresh curly parsley
2 bay leaves
4 black peppercorns, or ¼ teaspoon fine black pepper
2 to 3 teaspoons salt

1. Preheat oven to 400°F. Place chicken in cool salted water for few minutes to remove excess blood. Rinse well. Place chicken, celery, carrots, onion, and garlic in large roasting pan. Sprinkle salt and pepper lightly over chicken and vegetables. Roast in oven, turning occasionally, for 1 hour or a little longer. Chicken should be browned and caramelized.

2. Transfer chicken, vegetables, and juice left in pan, to an 8-quart heavy stockpot. Add the water, enough to cover chicken. Add the parsley, bay leaves, peppercorns, and salt. Bring pot to boiling. Skim foam from top of pot often, until foam subsides. Cook chicken over simmering heat until meat falls off the bones and bones separate, about 2 hours and 30 minutes. Remove chicken and vegetables, squeezing out any excess broth and discard. Strain broth through mesh colander. Broth should have a rich chicken flavor and will yield about 10 cups.

3. Cool, place in containers in refrigerator overnight. Soup should be congealed the next day. Skim hardened fat off top of soup and discard. Store in heavy 1-quart freezer bags, 1 to 2 cups in each. Use as called for in soup recipes, or meat or vegetable dishes. This soup is largely unattended and can be made while you get other things done.

Minestrone Soup

NOTE: *This is a classic Italian soup, one to be eaten with crusty Italian bread for dipping. The chicken broth gives a wonderful flavor, and the crushed red pepper gives it a boost. These vegetables are just my version, but most any will work in this soup.*

4 ounces pancetta, chopped, ½ cup

3 tablespoons olive oil

1 medium onion, chopped

2 cloves garlic, chopped

2 cups celery

1 cup carrots, peeled and chopped

1 cup potatoes,
unpeeled and small quartered

4 cups cabbage, chopped small

1 teaspoon salt

¼ teaspoon ground black pepper

1 (28-ounce) can whole tomatoes, chopped,
juice included

6 cups homemade or low-sodium canned
chicken broth

2 cans cannellini beans, drained and rinsed

1 bay leaf

2 tablespoons fresh Italian flat-leaf parsley

½ teaspoon crushed red pepper flakes

½ teaspoon dried basil

1 teaspoon salt

¼ teaspoon ground black pepper

1 small tender zucchini, unpeeled,
chopped small, about 1 cup

½ cup ditali pasta

extra water if needed

Parmesan cheese for garnish

1. Pour the olive oil in a large saucepan and fry the pancetta 3 to 4 minutes, turning often. Add the onion and garlic, and sauté together for about 5 minutes. Add the celery, carrot, and potato and continue to stir-fry for a few more minutes. Add the cabbage and salt and pepper the vegetables. Continue frying, another 5 to 6 minutes, until the vegetables become crisp-tender. Add the tomatoes and cook until heated through, another 5 minutes.

2. Transfer the vegetables to an 8-quart pot. Add the chicken broth, beans, bay leaf, parsley, crushed red pepper flakes, basil, and salt and pepper. Bring soup to a soft boil and let simmer for about 40 minutes. The vegetables should be soft, but not mushy. Add the zucchini and the pasta together. Cook for an additional 7 minutes. Add additional water if soup is too thick, starting with a half cup at a time. Taste and add any additional seasoning if you like. Ladle soup into small pasta bowls and garnish with freshly grated Parmesan cheese. Serves 8.

Minestrone Soup

Rosalie's Italian Lentil Soup
(WITH ITALIAN MEAT AND SAUSAGE)

NOTE: *This is a classic Italian soup and can be served as first course with most Italian meals. After refrigeration, this soup becomes very thick; thin with water and serve. It becomes better the next day.*

6 cups homemade or low-sodium chicken broth

2 cups water, more if needed

2 cups lentils, inspected, washed, and drained

¾ pound ground chuck

1 tablespoon plain bread crumbs

1 tablespoon grated Parmesan cheese

1 large clove garlic, chopped

1 tablespoon fresh Italian flat-leaf parsley, chopped

½ teaspoon salt

¼ teaspoon ground black pepper

¼ teaspoon fennel seed

1 egg

1 link Italian sausage

½ cup olive oil (divided)

1 small onion, chopped

1 large clove garlic, chopped

½ cup carrots, peeled and diced

½ cup celery, diced

½ cup tomatoes, diced

1 teaspoon salt

¼ teaspoon ground black pepper

½ teaspoon dried basil

¼ teaspoon dried oregano

⅛ teaspoon cumin

grated Parmesan cheese for garnish

1. In large stockpot, add 6 cups chicken broth, plus 2 cups water. Add washed drained lentils and put on medium heat.

2. Mix together in a bowl the ground chuck, bread crumbs, cheese, garlic, parsley, salt, pepper, fennel seed, and egg. Remove casing from Italian sausage.

3. Brown the ground chuck mixture and sausage together in 1/4 cup olive oil until lightly browned. Drain meat on paper towel and add crumbled meat to lentils.

4. In large saucepan, add ¼ cup olive oil and sauté together the onion, garlic, carrot, and celery. Fry 6 to 8 minutes, until onions are translucent. Add the vegetables to lentils.

5. Next add the diced tomatoes, salt, pepper, basil, oregano, and cumin. Stir together well.

6. Simmer lentils about 45 minutes, until tender. Test for taste. Add more salt and pepper if desired. Add an additional ½ to 1 cup water if soup becomes too thick. Serve soup in bowls garnished with Parmesan cheese. Serves 6 to 8.

(Time: 1 Hour and 30 Minutes)

Italian Beef Soup
(WITH MEATBALLS)

NOTE: *My mother, Ann Fiorino, would make this soup almost every week in the winter. We always looked forward to it and would dip her fresh Italian bread in the broth. A wonderful comfort food!*

6 cups homemade or low-sodium canned beef broth

2 cups water

½ pound stew meat

salt and pepper

¼ cup olive oil

1 pound ground chuck

¼ cup plain bread crumbs

¼ cup grated Parmesan cheese

¼ cup finely chopped onion

2 eggs

2 tablespoons fresh Italian flat-leaf parsley, chopped

1 teaspoon salt

¼ teaspoon ground black pepper

2 cups celery with leaves, sliced ¼"

⅔ cup carrot, peeled and sliced ¼"

1 small onion, chopped

1 medium potato, unpeeled, quartered small

1 (15-ounce) can diced tomatoes, juice included

½ pound acini di pepe pasta

salt

coarse ground black pepper

freshly grated Parmesan cheese for garnish

1. Using an 8-quart pot, add the beef broth and water to make 8 cups liquid, and bring to soft boil. Salt and pepper stew meat and brown in olive oil about 15 minutes. Place in soup stock.

2. Combine ground chuck, bread crumbs, cheese, onion, eggs, parsley, and salt and pepper. Mix together well. Form into small meatballs and drop into boiling broth. Skim foam from meatballs, as it rises to the top.

3. Add celery, carrot, onion, potato, and tomatoes. Cover pot and simmer on low heat about 45 minutes or until vegetables are tender.

4. Add acini di pepe directly to the soup; simmer an additional 10 to 12 minutes. Add salt and pepper to taste. Pour into soup bowls. Garnish with grated Parmesan cheese. Serves 4 to 6.

DANA HARPOLE SCHULTZ WITH ROSALIE

(Time: 1 Hour and 45 Minutes)

Minestra Maritata
(ITALIAN WEDDING SOUP)

NOTE: *This soup is popular at Italian-American weddings; however the term "wedding soup" is not found in Italy. The name possibly came from the marriage of "meat and greens" and how well meatballs and escarole taste together. I can only describe this soup as "simply wonderful."*

5 quarts water

1 whole soup chicken

3 stalks celery with leaves, cut in halves

2 medium carrots, peeled and halved

1 medium onion, halved

2 to 3 sprigs parsley, curly or Italian

1 tablespoon salt

¼ teaspoon ground black pepper

Tiny Meatballs recipe as found on page 54

1 head chopped escarole, about 4 cups

½ pound acini di pepe pasta

coarse ground black pepper

freshly grated Parmesan cheese for garnish

1. In an 8-quart pot, add 5 quarts water. Rinse chicken under cool water and place in pot with celery, carrots, onion, parsley sprigs, and salt and pepper. Bring to boil and skim off foam as it rises to the top. Cover with lid and cook 1 hour or longer, until the chicken is tender.

2. Remove chicken to platter and let cool completely. Remove vegetables from broth and discard. Bring broth to soft boil and make tiny meatballs, about the size of large grapes.

3. Drop meatballs into hot broth and skim any foam from meatballs as it rises to top of broth. Skin and debone cooled chicken. Cut into small cubes and return to broth. Let the meatballs and chicken cook together about 10 minutes. Rinse the escarole and remove bottom core. Chop and add to broth. Keep broth on soft boil and simmer together, 5 minutes.

4. Add the acini di pepe pasta and cook until pasta is tender, about 10 minutes. Pepper soup as desired. This broth should have a rich chicken and beef flavor. Ladle soup into small bowls; garnish with freshly grated Parmesan cheese if desired. Serves 8 to 10.

Italian Wedding Soup

Tiny Meatballs
(USED IN WEDDING SOUP)

NOTE: *These are easy to make and freeze well in heavy 1-quart freezer bags. Keep some on hand for adding to your homemade soups.*

Minestra Maritata (Italian Wedding Soup) recipe found on pages 52 and 53

1 pound ground chuck
¼ cup plain bread crumbs
¼ cup grated Parmesan cheese
1 clove garlic, chopped
2 tablespoons parsley, Italian or curly, chopped
2 eggs
1 teaspoon salt
⅛ teaspoon ground black pepper

1. Combine all ingredients and make into small meatballs, (the size of large grapes). Bring the broth to boil and drop the meatballs into hot broth until all meatballs have been used. Skim foam from meatballs as it rises to the top. Simmer about 20 minutes. These meatballs give much flavor in Italian soups.

(Time: 5 Minutes)

Italian Salad Dressing

NOTE: *For coarse ground pepper, look for Tone's Restaurant Black Pepper, sold at Sam's Club. You can double or triple this recipe and always have salad dressing available. Keep at room temperature.*

¾ cup extra virgin or mild, olive oil

¼ cup red wine vinegar

1 tablespoon balsamic vinegar

1 teaspoon coarse sea salt

½ to 1 teaspoon coarse ground black pepper

1. Mix the olive oil, vinegars, and seasonings in a jar with lid. Shake well and serve the desired amount on salads, or use for dipping Italian bread.

ROSALIE SERVING SALAD AT A CHARITY BENEFIT

Italian Salad

NOTE: *Rope provel cheese can be found at most well-known grocers in the cheese deli. Sea salt has a brighter flavor and you will enjoy this change. Other additives may include marinated artichoke hearts, pimentos, and chopped Genoa salami.*

1 pound bag Iceberg lettuce, with red cabbage and carrots added

1 large bunch red or green leaf lettuce

⅔ cup grape tomatoes

½ cup olives, your choice of black, green, or kalamata, pitted

½ cup tender celery hearts, chopped

4 to 6 pepperoncini peppers (optional)

¾ cup extra virgin or mild, olive oil

¼ cup red wine vinegar

1 tablespoon balsamic vinegar

1 teaspoon coarse sea salt, or more for taste

½ teaspoon coarse ground black pepper

6 to 8 slices purple onion rings

2 cups rope Provel cheese if available

   or ½ cup freshly grated Parmesan

1. Place the bag of iceberg lettuce in large bowl. Set aside. Rinse leaf lettuce, drain, and pat dry; cut into 3" pieces. Add leaf lettuce to the iceberg lettuce, along with the tomatoes, olives, celery, and pepperoncini peppers, if using. Toss together.

2. In a jar with lid, add the olive oil, vinegars, coarse sea salt, and pepper. Shake together well and add as much dressing as desired on the salad.

3. Garnish top of salad with red onion rings and rope provel cheese if available or top with grated Parmesan. Serves 4 to 6.

Red Pepper Infused Olive Oil
(FOR DIPPING OR DRESSING)

NOTE: *This flavored spicy oil is wonderful and great to dip bread. Use it alone or in combination with other dressings over salad. It is especially good drizzled over raw vegetables, such as broccoli and cauliflower.*

1 cup extra virgin or mild, olive oil
2 teaspoons crushed red pepper flakes
½ teaspoon coarse sea salt

1. Place oil and crushed red pepper flakes in a small heavy saucepan. Heat together over medium heat about 5 minutes, stirring constantly. The oil will become fragrant. Remove from heat, add salt and stir. Cool to room temperature (about 2 hours) before using. Transfer to oil flask with cork and seal. Keep with other oils in cool place. Makes 1 cup.

(Time: 15 Minutes)

Broccoli & Cauliflower Salad

NOTE: *A wonderful light salad that is especially good in the summer with barbecue.*

2 cups broccoli florets
2 cups cauliflower florets
⅓ cup chopped green onions, tops included
½ cup chopped celery, leaves included
¼ cup Spanish olives with pimiento
⅓ cup Genoa chunk hard salami, small cubed, optional

Italian Salad Dressing Recipe found on page 55

1. Combine all ingredients in a large bowl. Prepare Italian salad dressing and pour over salad. Toss together well and chill until ready to serve. Serves 6.

Greek Salad

NOTE: *If you are not a fan of feta cheese, omit and garnish with ½ cup Pecorino Romano, or use both if you desire. This is a great salad for a crowd. Use a sweet balsamic, such as Balsamic Vinegar of Modena.*

1 (16-ounce) bag spring-mix baby lettuce leaves, freshly cleaned and air-dried
1 bunch romaine lettuce, washed and drained
1 cup Kalamata olives, drained
8 pepperoncini peppers, drained
1 small cucumber, unpeeled and sliced thin
⅔ cup grape tomatoes

⅔ cup extra virgin olive oil
⅓ cup sweet balsamic vinegar
1 teaspoon coarse sea salt, or more to taste
½ to 1 teaspoon freshly ground coarse black pepper

⅔ cup crumbled feta cheese
½ cup **Garlic Herbed Croutons** recipe found on page 108

1. In large bowl, empty bag of spring mix. Rinse off romaine and squeeze out any left-over water and pat dry. Chop the romaine coarsely and add to spring mix. Toss the greens together and add the Kalamata olives, pepperoncinis, cucumber, and grape tomatoes.

2. In a jar with lid, add the olive oil, vinegar, and salt and pepper. Shake together well and pour over salad, using all or as much dressing as desired. Toss the salad with clean hands until well coated with dressing.

3. Garnish top with feta cheese and garlic croutons. Taste and add additional salt or pepper if desired. Serves 8.

Salmon Spinach Salad

(Time: 20 Minutes)

Salmon Spinach Salad

NOTE: *This dish is a meal in itself and is very delicious and attractive to serve. For a different variation, use garlic sautéed sliced chicken breasts. (See **Garlic Sautéed Chicken** recipe found
on page 185.)*

4 salmon fillets, 1½" thick

¼ cup butter, melted

¼ cup extra virgin olive oil

2 tablespoons freshly squeezed lemon juice

1 teaspoon coarse garlic salt with dried parsley

olive oil

coarse garlic salt with dried parsley

1 (10-ounce) package fresh spinach, stems removed, washed and patted dry

1 cup whole walnuts, divided

1 cup sun-dried tomatoes, divided

1 cup fresh quartered tomatoes, divided

2 cups rope Provel cheese, divided

 or freshly shredded provolone cheese

1 cup white capped mushrooms, thick sliced, divided

¾ cup extra virgin olive oil

¼ cup red wine vinegar

1 tablespoon sweet balsamic vinegar

1 teaspoon coarse sea salt

½ teaspoon freshly ground coarse black pepper

1. Preheat oven to 475°F. Mix butter, olive oil, lemon juice, and garlic salt in a jar with lid. Shake
   well to blend.

2. Coat a foiled-covered baking pan with olive oil. Lay the salmon fillets on the pan. Pierce each
   fillet with a fork in several places. Pour olive oil/butter mixture evenly over the 4 salmon fillets,
   and sprinkle liberally with coarse garlic salt. Roast uncovered, 6 to 7 minutes on each side, until the salmon is pink and flakes easily. Remove from oven and cut away the thick bottom skin
   from each fillet with a sharp knife and discard. Set aside. Pour pan juices over the fillets.

(Salmon Spinach Salad . . . continued on page 62)

(Salmon Spinach Salad . . . continued from page 61)

3. In 4 large salad bowls, divide the spinach, using 4 cups loosely packed spinach leaves per bowl. Divide the walnuts, sun-dried tomatoes, fresh tomatoes, rope Provel, and mushrooms among the four bowls, spreading ¼ cup each item plus ½ cup of the Provel cheese over top of each bowl.

4. Place the olive oil, vinegars, and salt and pepper in a jar with lid and shake well. Divide and pour the dressing over each spinach salad. Lay each cooked salmon fillet over the top center of each salad.

5. If more dressing is needed, double the batch. Serves 4 meal-sized salads or 8 small salads.

Insalata Caprese Salad
(TOMATO AND MOZZARELLA SALAD)

NOTE: *Insalata Caprese comes from the Isle of Capri and is one of the most popular of Italian summer salads. If possible, use only vine-ripened tomatoes and fresh grown basil for the most flavor. The colors are symbolic of Italy; red, white, and green.*

½ pound fresh mozzarella cheese, drained and sliced ¼", then quartered

2 large fresh vine-ripened tomatoes, small quartered

  or 1 cup cherry tomatoes, halved

1 cup fresh basil leaves, torn in pieces

⅓ cup extra virgin olive oil

2 tablespoons fresh squeezed lemon juice

1 teaspoon coarse sea salt, or more for taste

⅛ teaspoon freshly ground coarse black pepper, or more for taste

1. Place the mozzarella, tomatoes, and basil leaves in a medium bowl. Whisk together the olive oil, lemon juice, and salt and pepper. Pour dressing over salad and toss together. Test for taste, adding more salt or pepper if desired. Serve with or over Italian bread slices. Serves 4.

Italian Green Bean Salad

Italian Green Bean Salad

NOTE: *This is a popular Italian summer salad, and a tasty way to make green beans. This dish is very pretty in a large white bowl and is just as delicious. This is a great salad to accompany a barbecue.*

2 pounds fresh green beans, ends trimmed and left whole
5 to 6 new potatoes, unpeeled and small quartered or halved
3 teaspoons salt

1 large yellow onion, sliced thin
2 cloves garlic, minced
2 large fresh tomatoes, cored and quartered

½ cup extra virgin or mild, olive oil
¼ cup cider vinegar
1 teaspoon coarse sea salt, or more if desired.
¼ teaspoon freshly ground coarse black pepper

1. Wash green beans. In large pot, boil green beans and potatoes together with salt added, 15 to 20 minutes, until green beans are tender and potatoes are done. Drain green beans with potatoes and transfer to large bowl. While still warm, add onions, garlic, and tomatoes.

2. Whisk together the olive oil, vinegar, and salt and pepper. Toss together well. Serve warm with any meat entree. Serves 6.

Italian Stuffed Tomatoes

NOTE: *A light summer lunch to serve with your favorite soup and Italian bread.*

4 large, fresh, firm garden tomatoes

2 cans tuna, packed in olive oil

½ cup chopped tomatoes, made from scooped out tomatoes

½ cup tender celery hearts, with leaves

¼ cup chopped green onions, tops included

2 large boiled eggs, chopped

¼ cup stuffed green olives with pimento

⅓ cup fresh chopped basil leaves

1 teaspoon red wine vinegar

lettuce leaves

sun-dried tomatoes for garnish

1. Cut tops off tomatoes crosswise, about ½" down. Gently scoop out inside of tomato, leaving side and bottom margin to support filling. Pour the undrained tuna into large mixing bowl. Add the chopped tomatoes, celery, onions, eggs, olives, basil leaves, and vinegar.

2. Mix together and spoon back into tomatoes, filling to a little over the top. Serve tomatoes on lettuce leaves, garnish with 2 to 3 sun-dried tomatoes. Serves 4.

Tomatoes

Awesome Potato Salad

NOTE: *This was my mother, Ann Fiorino's, version of potato salad. It has been handed down to her daughters, and granddaughters. We just couldn't make it any other way. This is very smooth and so delicious, especially when served warm. Everyone will want this recipe.*

5 pounds red potatoes
2 teaspoons salt
6 hard boiled eggs, chopped

⅓ cup onion, chopped
⅔ cup tender celery hearts, with leaves, chopped
1 quart Kraft Miracle Whip, or your favorite salad dressing
1 teaspoon yellow mustard
1 teaspoon salt
½ teaspoon fine ground black pepper

2 slices bacon
2 teaspoons red wine vinegar
1 teaspoon sugar
paprika to sprinkle
parsley sprigs to garnish

1. Wash and peel potatoes. Cut into small quarters, about 1" pieces. Boil potatoes in an 8-quart pot in salted water, until potatoes are tender but not mushy. Boil eggs until hard boiled. Remove when done and set aside. Drain cooked potatoes and place in large mixing bowl. Peel eggs when cooled; chop and add to warm potatoes. Add the onion, celery, salad dressing, mustard, salt, and pepper.

2. Cook the bacon until crispy and remove from heat. Remove all but 1 tablespoon of the bacon drippings. Crunch the bacon up into small pieces and add back to bacon dripping. Add the vinegar and sugar and put back on heat for about 30 seconds to form thin syrup. Add all at once to the potato salad. Mix together until well blended. Sprinkle top with paprika and garnish top of salad with parsley sprigs. Serves 12.

(Time: 15 Minutes)

Cannellini Bean Salad

NOTE: *This is dish well known in Tuscany, usually served over a bed of tender arugula. If you can find arugula, by all means use it. However, I think it works just as well over romaine lettuce. The beans taste creamy in this salad and some can be slightly crushed. This is a good Italian salad for anytime lunch.*

2 (6-ounce) cans tuna packed in olive oil

2 (15-ounce) cans cannellini beans, drained and rinsed

1 medium red onion, thinly sliced

⅔ cup grape tomatoes

¼ cup basil leaves, shredded

4 to 5 cups romaine lettuce, chopped

¼ cup extra virgin olive oil

¼ cup red wine vinegar

¼ teaspoon crushed red pepper flakes

1½ teaspoons coarse sea salt

½ teaspoon freshly ground coarse black pepper

Italian bread slices, toasted

1. Spoon tuna out into large salad bowl, breaking up any large chunks. Rinse and drain the cannellini beans and add to the tuna. Add the onion, tomatoes, basil leaves, and lettuce and mix together.

2. Put the olive oil, vinegar, red pepper flakes, and salt and pepper in a jar with a lid. Shake well and pour over salad. Toss well; serve over Italian toasted bread slices. Makes 8 side salads.

Stuffed
Zucchini
with
Couscous

Vegetables and Side Dishes

Vegetables Italiano: In the Italian culture, vegetables are prepared with almost every meal. My mother, who descended from Sicily, would tell me that when she was a child growing up, to have meat at a meal was a treat. It was mostly saved for Sunday. Because families were usually large, and vegetables and legumes were plentiful, many weekday meals were made up of pasta with vegetables; such as pasta with asparagus, broccoli, peas, and beans. Of course, vegetables can be a meal served alone. I can remember my mother going out every spring with her little knife and picking up dandelions. She would bring in a big bag and wash them in the sink over and over. She would boil them until tender, put them in a bowl dressed with olive oil and garlic, add a little salt and pepper and you would have thought she was in heaven. She would always have vegetables cooked in garlic and olive oil on the stove. And what Italian kitchen would be without tomatoes, peppers, artichokes, eggplants, zucchini, or cauliflower, just to name a few?

Side Dishes or Meals: I cannot think of many vegetables that cannot be sautéed, braised, or even roasted in the oven with a little olive oil and garlic. Topped with Parmesan cheese or bread crumbs, Italians have created perfectly wonderful side dishes. On the other hand, some vegetables have become an Italian-American craze and a meal in itself. Think of *Eggplant Rollatini, Stuffed Artichokes,* or *Italian Stuffed Peppers.*

Dressed Simple or Class Act: As mentioned before, what makes vegetables Italian is the olive oil and garlic. For a little taste of everything, try the *Caponata*, which has several vegetables all marinated in a sweet sour sauce. *Pasta Primavera,* is very popular and offers both pasta and vegetables together. Use the freshest vegetables available for the best results.

Additional Tips: Salting the vegetables while they are frying in the pan causes them to release moisture, bringing out the flavor of the vegetables. Be careful not to overcook the vegetables. They should be tender but not mushy. And lastly if possible, plant some herbs in your backyard or grow them in your house under a grow-light. Fresh herbs will boost the flavor in your dishes and you will love the results.

Stuffed Zucchini with Couscous

NOTE: *This is a great dish full of flavor and very attractive. Serve the zucchini whole for a main meal course or cut in portions for a side dish. This is especially good in the summer when zucchini are plentiful.*

2 medium zucchini,
   stems removed and halved lengthwise
3 tablespoons olive oil, divided
I small zucchini, cut into 1" pieces
1 medium onion, chopped small
2 cloves garlic, chopped fine

2½ cups homemade or
   low-sodium chicken broth
1 cup couscous

12 cherry tomatoes
8 fresh basil leaves, shredded
1 tablespoon toasted pine nuts
   or chopped walnuts
1 teaspoon salt
¼ teaspoon ground black pepper

crushed red pepper flakes for garnish
grated Parmesan cheese for garnish

1. Preheat oven to 375°F. Rinse zucchini under cool water. Pat dry and remove ends. Cut zucchinis in half lengthwise. Place halved-sized down on lightly oiled baking sheet and bake until soft, 10 to 12 minutes. Remove and cool.

2. Scoop out centers of the zucchini leaving ¼" thickness in shells. Place scooped-out zucchini in large fry pan with 2 tablespoons olive oil. Add the small chopped zucchini, onion, and garlic. Sauté altogether until lightly browned, 5 to 6 minutes. Add the chicken broth, couscous and remaining 1 tablespoon olive oil. Bring to boil and cook together about 3 minutes.

3. Add tomatoes, basil leaves, pine nuts, or walnuts and salt and pepper. Then stir together.

4. Fill zucchini shells with couscous mixture and place in 13" x 9" baking dish, lightly coated with olive oil. Cover with aluminum foil and bake in oven for 15 to 20 minutes until set.

5. Remove from oven and garnish with crushed red pepper flakes and freshly grated cheese. Cut stuffed zucchini into halves. Serves 8.

Eggplant Rollatini

NOTE: *I can't describe how delicious these are. You will just have to experience them for yourself. You can purchase a small meat slicer or a mandoline in kitchen specialty shops. The slices should be thin, but not to the point of falling apart.*

1 large eggplant, about 4" diameter
1 tablespoon salt

1 cup Progresso Italian Style bread crumbs
½ cup grated Parmesan cheese
2 cloves garlic, minced
2 tablespoons fresh Italian flat-leaf parsley, chopped

3 eggs, beaten
salt and pepper

1 (15-ounce) carton ricotta cheese
1 cup mozzarella cheese, shredded thin
½ cup Pecorino Romano or Parmesan cheese
1/4 cup fresh Italian flat-leaf parsley, chopped
1 egg
⅛ teaspoon black ground pepper

⅓ cup olive oil for frying, or more as needed
Marinara Sauce recipe found on page 127
½ cup grated Parmesan cheese

1. Preheat oven to 375°F. Cut stem and end from eggplant. Peel the eggplant partially in strips, leaving some of the peel intact. Using a meat cutter or a mandoline, slice the eggplant into thin lengthwise slices, about ⅛" thick. Let the eggplant slices soak in cool water with 1 tablespoon salt added for about 30 minutes while you prepare the other steps.

2. Place the bread crumbs, cheese, garlic, and parsley in a shallow plate. Beat the eggs until fluffy.

3. Prepare the filling by placing the ricotta, mozzarella, Pecorino Romano, parsley, egg, and pepper in a bowl. Mix well and set aside.

   (Eggplant Rollatini . . . continued on Page 74)

(Eggplant Rollatini . . . continued from Page 73)

4. Rinse the eggplant in cool water and drain. Dip each slice in the beaten eggs and then the bread crumbs on both sides. Place the olive oil in a large skillet and over medium heat, fry the eggplant about 2 minutes on each side until golden. Salt and pepper lightly as they fry. Drain slices on paper towels. Add olive oil to pan as needed, and if necessary, start a clean pan midway of frying.

5. Meanwhile, using a 13" x 9" baking dish, pour in 1 cup marinara sauce to cover the bottom. When all of the eggplant slices have been fried and drained, place them on a large cookie sheet. Place 2 tablespoons ricotta filling on each slice, and spread gently. Starting from the short end of the slice, roll the eggplant up jelly-roll style. Place each roll, seam-side down, in the baking dish. You should have about 15 rolls. If all the rolls do not fit, use an additional smaller dish.

6. Pour the remaining sauce, an additional 3 to 4 cups over the rolls. Top with the Parmesan cheese. Cover loosely with aluminum foil. Bake about 30 minutes, until bubbly on the sides. Serves 4 to 6.

Eggplant Rollatini

Italian Roasted Vegetables

NOTE: *These vegetables can also be put on a skewer on the grill in summer months. Dip them in the olive mixture and season. Variation: Top with shredded mozzarella or feta cheese for a Greek touch. This is great for side dish or appetizer.*

1 red bell pepper
1 yellow bell pepper
1 green bell pepper
1 small green zucchini
1 small yellow zucchini
2 large onions, peeled and quartered
8 large white button mushrooms, whole
½ pound asparagus, hard ends
  trimmed and halved
3 to 4 small new potatoes,
  halved or left whole

3 cloves garlic, chopped
6 to 8 fresh basil leaves, chopped
  or ½ teaspoon dried

½ cup olive oil
1 to 2 teaspoons coarse sea salt
ground black pepper to taste

1 cup cherry tomatoes
coarse garlic salt with dried parsley
coarse ground black pepper to taste

1 to 2 tablespoons balsamic vinegar
crushed red pepper flakes for garnish
Pecorino Romano cheese, for garnish
olive oil

1. Preheat oven to 450° F. Remove stems and seed from peppers, then cut in 2" strips. Trim ends of zucchinis and cut into 2" rounds. Place peppers and zucchinis along with other trimmed and cut vegetables in large roasting pan.

2. Mix together garlic, basil, olive oil, salt, and pepper. Pour mixture over vegetables and toss until well coated. Place in hot oven and roast, turning vegetables once or twice, 25 to 30 minutes. Vegetables should be soft but not mushy. Add a little more olive oil if vegetables appear too dry.

3. Add cherry tomatoes about 5 minutes before completing roasting. Remove vegetables from oven. Sprinkle a little garlic salt and pepper to taste over vegetables. Transfer vegetables to large platter.

4. Sprinkle balsamic vinegar over hot vegetables and garnish as desired with crushed red pepper flakes and Pecorino Romano cheese. Pass additional olive oil at table for drizzling, if desired. Makes 6 to 8 servings.

Golden Fried Cauliflower

NOTE: *This dish is so simple to make and so delicious. Your guests will be raving about it all the way home.*

1 large head cauliflower, trimmed and broken into small florets
⅓ cup olive oil, or more if needed
3 cloves garlic, chopped
1 to 2 teaspoons salt
¼ teaspoon ground black pepper
2 to 3 tablespoons water
freshly grated Parmesan cheese for garnish

1. Wash cauliflower and remove hard core and stems up to where florets begin. Break pods into small florets, cutting some in half if still too large. Pour olive oil into large saucepan and sauté the garlic and florets together. Continue to stir-fry the cauliflower over medium heat 10 to 12 minutes, adding more olive oil if pan gets dry. The cauliflower should begin to get golden and crusty.

2. Sprinkle salt and pepper over the cauliflower while frying. When the cauliflower is crusty, add 2 to 3 tablespoons water to saucepan and put lid on pan to steam for about 2 minutes.

3. Taste; add more salt and pepper if desired. Cauliflower should be golden colored, crusted, and tender but not mushy. Remove to platter and garnish with cheese. Serves 6.

(Time: 5 Minutes)

Sautéed Spinach with Garlic

NOTE: *So simple, yet so delicious. The coarse sea salt is a must for this dish.*

¼ cup olive oil

3 cloves garlic, chopped

1 (9 ounce) bag fresh spinach, pre-washed and air-dried

½ teaspoon coarse sea salt, or more if desired

¼ teaspoon coarse ground back pepper

grated Parmesan cheese for garnish

1. In a large saucepan, sauté the garlic in olive oil until golden, about 1 minute. Place the spinach over the olive oil and add the salt and pepper. Heat together about 2 minutes, until the spinach is wilted but still firm. Garnish with cheese if desired. Serves 4.

Zesty Italian Zucchini

NOTE: *Fresh small zucchinis right out of the garden are great for this dish. They are tender, without so many seeds. However, you can still get good results with larger ones cooked the same way.*

3 to 4 small zucchinis, green and yellow, unpeeled and sliced¼" thick
¼ cup olive oil
1 medium onion, peeled and sliced ⅛" thick
3 cloves garlic, chopped
½ teaspoon salt, or more for taste
¼ teaspoon ground black pepper
2 tablespoons freshly squeezed lemon juice, about ½ lemon
additional salt and pepper to taste

1. Rinse zucchini in water; pat dry and trim ends. Cut into slices and place in large saucepan with olive oil, onion, and garlic. Stir-fry over medium heat 8 to 10 minutes. Salt and pepper while frying. At end of cooking, squeeze fresh lemon juice over zucchini and put lid on pan. Let steam for about 1 minute. Remove to platter. Add additional salt and pepper to taste. This dish is good hot or at room temperature. Serves 4.

Eggplant Parmigiana

NOTE: *This is a classic Italian dish, very simple and easy to make. Serve right out of baking dish on table. Good with warm Italian bread and butter.*

large eggplant, about 4" diameter,
  cut into ¼" round slices

1 tablespoon salt

1 cup Progresso Italian Style bread crumbs

½ cup grated Pecorino Romano cheese

2 cloves garlic, minced

2 tablespoons fresh Italian
  flat-leaf parsley, chopped

3 eggs beaten

⅓ cup olive oil for frying, or more as needed

salt and pepper

4 cups ***Marinara Sauce*** recipe found
  on page 127

1⅓ cups grated Parmesan cheese, divided

¼ cup fresh basil leaves, cut into strips

1 cup mozzarella cheese, shredded

freshly ground coarse black pepper

1. Preheat oven to 375°F. Cut stem and end from eggplant. Peel eggplant partially in strips, leaving some of the peel intact. Slice the eggplant thin, about ¼" thick, in round slices. This can be done by hand, mandoline, or small meat slicer. Let the eggplant slices soak in cool water with 1 tablespoon salt for about 30 minutes while you prepare the other steps.

2. Place the bread crumbs, cheese, garlic, and parsley in a shallow plate. Beat the eggs well and set aside. Rinse the eggplant in cool water, drain, and pat dry. Dip the eggplant slices in the eggs and then the bread crumbs on both sides. Place olive oil in a large saucepan over medium heat. Fry the eggplant 2 to 3 minutes on each side until golden. Salt and pepper lightly as they fry. Drain slices on paper towels. Add olive oil to pan as needed, or if necessary, start a clean pan midway through frying.

3. Prepare marinara sauce, or use a ready-made brand of your choice. Using a 13" x 9"baking dish, pour 1 cup sauce on bottom of pan. Lay ⅓ of the eggplant slices over the sauce. Next, sprinkle ⅓ cup Parmesan cheese over the slices. Continue, until last layer. Top the last layer with the basil leaves and mozzarella. Cover with aluminum foil loosely. Bake about 30 minutes, until bubbly on the sides.

4. Garnish with freshly ground coarse black pepper. Serves 6 to 8.

Italian Fried Cabbage

NOTE: *This is a favorite side dish that my husband and children love. They say it is as good as a plate of pasta. Although I don't know about that, I must say it is very delicious. It is a little fuss to make but definitely worth it. Don't worry if some of the slices fall apart. Just continue to coat the left-over pieces with egg and flour, then continue to fry.*

1 small head cabbage, quartered (cut in half, and then in half again)

6 cups water

2 teaspoons salt

1 cup flour

¼ cup grated Parmesan cheese

1 teaspoon coarse garlic salt with dried parsley

¼ teaspoon ground black pepper

3 eggs, beaten

1 cup olive oil for frying, more or less

Marinara Sauce recipe found on page 127

1 cup freshly grated Parmesan cheese, divided

freshly ground coarse black pepper

1. Boil cabbage in large pot with 6 cups water and salt, until cabbage is tender. Drain cabbage and let cool. Put cabbage on cutting board, and slice into ½" slices, trying to keep slices together.

2. Mix flour, cheese, garlic salt, and pepper, and put into large shallow plate. Gently lay cabbage slices into beaten eggs, and lift out with slotted spatula to drain. Place in seasoned flour, turning to coat both sides. Using a heavy large saucepan, fry cabbage in hot oil 2 to 3 minutes on each side, until golden crusted. Remove fried slices to baking pan. Continue to fry until all slices and pieces of cabbage are used, adding olive oil as you go along.

3. Arrange some of the slices in a single layer on a large platter. Cover with part of sauce and grated cheese. Continue with layers of cabbage, one on top of the other, as in a layered casserole, adding sauce and cheese over each layer.

4. Garnish last layer with remaining cheese and freshly ground coarse black pepper. Serves 4 to 6.

Italian Fried Peppers

NOTE: *These peppers are so good. They can be used to top Italian sandwiches, such as hamburgers or grilled chicken.*

1 red bell pepper
1 yellow bell pepper
1 green bell pepper
¼ cup olive oil
2 cloves garlic, chopped
salt and pepper

1 (8-ounce) can tomato sauce
1 tablespoon water
½ teaspoon sugar

1 teaspoon balsamic vinegar
salt and pepper to taste
grated Parmesan cheese for garnish

1. Wash, core, and seed peppers. Cut in julienne pieces, not too thin. Place peppers in saucepan with olive oil and garlic and sauté 8 to10 minutes until tender, but not mushy. Salt and pepper while frying. Add tomato sauce, water, and sugar. Cook together on low heat about 5 minutes.

2. Add the balsamic vinegar and stir. Continue to cook about 1 more minute. Taste, add more salt or pepper if desired. Transfer to a platter. Garnish with Parmesan cheese and serve with a meat entree. Serves 4 to 6.

Sautéed Brussels Sprouts

NOTE: *Brussels sprouts are miniature cabbages. The smaller the better is a good rule. They are wonderful sautéed in olive oil and garlic. Served well with Italian sausage or breaded cutlets. If using frozen brussels sprouts, boil 10 minutes, until tender.*

1 pound small fresh brussels sprouts
2 quarts water
1 teaspoon salt

⅓ cup olive oil
3 cloves garlic, chopped
½ teaspoon salt, or more for taste
⅛ teaspoon pepper

1. Wash and drain brussels sprouts. Place in 3-quart pot with 2 quarts water and salt. Bring to boil and cook brussels sprouts for 20 minutes, until tender. Drain well.

2. Place olive oil and garlic in saucepan. Sauté over medium heat for about 1 minute. Add the brussels sprouts and salt and pepper. With plastic spatula, cut the sprouts in half while in the pan. Fry, stirring occasionally until heated through, 6 to 8 minutes. Transfer to medium bowl. Serve hot. Serves 4.

Italian Roasted Potatoes

NOTE: *Small new potatoes in season are great for this dish. Cut the larger ones in half, but keep the smaller ones whole.*

¼ cup olive oil
1 tablespoon butter

3 cloves garlic, minced
1 tablespoon herbes de Provence
1 teaspoon coarse sea salt
¼ teaspoon ground black pepper

1 pound small unpeeled potatoes, brown or red
grated Parmesan cheese, for garnish

1. Preheat oven to 400°F. Place olive oil and butter in saucepan. Over medium heat, sauté the garlic in the olive oil and butter for 1 to 2 minutes, until garlic is slightly golden. Add the herbes de Provence and salt and pepper. Warm together, about 15 seconds. Remove from stove.

2. Wash and lightly scrub potatoes. In large bowl, mix the potatoes and olive oil/butter. Pierce the potatoes a few times with fork and place in a 9" round pan. Roast uncovered for 45 minutes, turning a few times. Garnish with grated cheese, if desired. Serves 4 to 6.

Boiled Herbed Potatoes

NOTE: *These boiled potatoes are very light and go well with most meat or fish entrees.*

1½ pounds small baby, or Yukon potatoes, quartered
2 teaspoons salt

½ stick butter
1 teaspoon garlic, minced, or more for taste
2 teaspoons fresh squeezed lemon juice
2 tablespoons Italian flat-leaf parsley, chopped
1 teaspoon coarse sea salt
⅛ teaspoon coarse black pepper, or more for taste
1 teaspoon herbes de Provence, optional

¼ cup grated Parmesan cheese
parsley sprigs

1. Wash and lightly scrub potatoes. Boil potatoes in salted water, about 15 minutes, until tender. Drain, reserving ¼ cup liquid. Return to low heat. Coarsely chop the potatoes. Sauté the garlic in butter, about 1 minute. Add the lemon juice, parsley, and salt and pepper. Add the herbes de Provence, if desired. Stir together to blend and pour over boiled potatoes.

2. Toss together well. Serve garnished with grated Parmesan cheese and parsley sprigs. Serves 6.

Braised Swiss Chard
(WITH GARLIC AND TOMATO)

NOTE: *I can remember eating this dish as a child. My mother always had a big pot of greens on the stove and this was one of my favorites.*

1 pound Swiss chard, stems removed
¼ cup olive oil
2 cloves garlic, chopped
½ teaspoon salt
¼ teaspoon ground black pepper

⅔ cup fresh tomatoes, chopped,
   or ⅔ cup canned diced tomatoes, juice included
¼ teaspoon sugar
1 cup water
salt and pepper to taste

1. Wash and rinse the Swiss chard three times in cold water to remove any dirt or sand. Trim ends and cut the long stalks in fourths. Place the olive oil in a large saucepan and sauté the garlic about 2 minutes, until it starts to turn golden. Add the Swiss chard, and salt and pepper while frying.

2. Add the tomatoes and sprinkle the sugar over the tomatoes. Add the water and steam the Swiss chard with lid on for about 15 minutes, until the greens are tender and the flavors are combined. Add a little more water if desired. Garnish with salt and pepper to your taste. Serves 4.

ROSALIE TEACHING HER GRANDDAUGHTER TAYLOR HARPOLE

Baked Artichoke Casserole

NOTE: *This dish is much like the **Stuffed Artichokes** recipe found on page 91, without the work. To make this a seafood dish, add 1 cup medium-sized cooked shrimp and ½ cup crabmeat in the bowl with butter and artichokes. Warm in saucepan for 2 to 3 minutes before placing in baking dish. Bake as directed.*

2 tablespoons butter, melted
2 (12-ounce) jars marinated artichoke hearts, drained

1 cup Progresso Italian Style bread crumbs
½ cup Pecorino Romano cheese
¼ cup fresh Italian flat-leaf parsley, chopped
2 cloves garlic, minced
¼ cup plus 1 tablespoon extra virgin olive oil

1. Preheat oven to 350° F. Pour the melted butter in a bowl. Drain the artichokes and place in bowl with butter. Toss together until the artichokes are well coated. Lay the buttered artichokes in a small shallow baking dish.

2. In a separate bowl, mix the bread crumbs, cheese, parsley, garlic, and olive oil. Place the bread crumb mixture over the artichokes, and bake for 15 to 20 minutes. The breadcrumbs should be golden toasted. Serves 4.

Cardoons
(ITALIAN BREADED STALKS)

NOTE: *These breaded stalks are very popular among Sicilians. We used to call them cardoonas. Swiss chard is a spring vegetable of very dark green leaves, with a red vein down the middle. The greens are tender, but the stalks, usually a deep red, can be tough. When steamed and breaded, however, they are very delicious.*

1 large bunch Swiss chard stalks, with leafy greens removed
2 teaspoons salt

2 eggs, beaten
1 cup **Italian Bread Crumbs** recipe found on page 94

⅓ cup olive oil, or more if needed
salt and pepper to taste
¼ cup grated Parmesan cheese

1. Wash and rinse the Swiss chard three times in cold water to remove any dirt or sand. Cut the stalks off to where the leafy greens begin. Save the greens for another time or cook them using the **Braised Swiss Chard** recipe found on page 87. Cut the stalks in 3" to 4" lengths and boil them in salted water 5 to 6 minutes, until tender.

2. Drain and gently flatten them. Dip the stalks in the beaten eggs and then on both sides in the bread crumbs.

3. Fry in olive oil until browned on both sides. Salt and pepper lightly while frying. Remove and drain on paper towel. Transfer to platter and garnish with grated cheese. Serves 3 to 4, depending how many stalks are available from one bunch.

(Time: 1 Hour and 15 Minutes)

Stuffed Artichokes

NOTE: *Italians love stuffed artichokes. With a slice of Italian bread, one could make a meal on them. If you are short on time use my* **Baked Artichoke Casserole** *recipe found on page 89, using marinated artichoke hearts.*

1 lemon, freshly squeezed
   in 4 cups cool water for dipping artichokes
4 large artichokes

3 tablespoons extra virgin olive oil, divided
2 cloves garlic, minced

1 cup plain bread crumbs
½ cup Pecorino Romano cheese
¼ cup Italian flat-leaf parsley, chopped
salt and pepper to taste

2 tablespoons additional lemon juice
additional olive oil

1. Preheat oven to 375°F. Cut the lemon in half and squeeze the juice into the cool water. Dip the artichokes from time to time to keep them from discoloration while you are preparing them. Keep them in the water and work with one artichoke at a time. Cut stem off artichoke so it will lay flat on bottom. Remove hard outer leaves, about 2 to 3 layers or more, until you get down to the leaves that are green only at the tip. Gently pull and spread the leaves outward to expose the purple tipped leaves at the very center. Pull out the purple-tipped leaves to expose the fuzzy choke below. With a small teaspoon, scrape away the choke all the way down to the artichoke heart. Sprinkle lemon water in and around the artichoke to prevent discoloration. Cut off the top third of the artichoke leaves using a strong serrated knife.

2. Prepare the filling: Place 1 tablespoon olive oil in skillet. Add the garlic and heat 1 minute. Add the bread crumbs and toast them 1 to 2 minutes, constantly stirring in pan. Remove to a bowl. Add the cheese, chopped parsley and 1 tablespoon olive oil. Mix together, adding a little salt and pepper. Mixture will feel oily. Gently spread the outside of the prepared artichoke leaves and place the bread crumb mixture between all the leaves working from outside in.

3. In baking dish, place the artichokes so they fit together nicely. Add 1/2" water, plus 1 tablespoon olive oil and 2 tablespoons of lemon juice to bottom of the dish. Cover the dish with aluminum foil and bake for 45 minutes. Remove to platter and serve. Drizzle with additional olive oil. Starting at the outer leaves, remove one at a time and eat them with the filling, discarding any part of the leaf that may be tough. Serves 4.

Breads and Pizza

It has been said that bread is the sustenance of life. By far it is the most frequently sold commodity in the grocery store. Everyone loves a good slice of bread or roll with their meal. Italians are probably the most celebrated bread makers of any culture. Going back to the ancient days of Rome and Bible times, people have always found a way to make bread. Now in our time, you can bake wonderful Italian bread in your own oven at home. Not only will you be thrilled with your achievement, but all who dine at your table will be blessed. Leftover bread can be just as delicious. The best toast in the world comes from day-old Italian bread. Other uses are croutons or hard bread for soups and for dipping in olive oil and tomatoes. The following are some things I learned from my mother, and from just plain experimenting.

Basic Ingredients: Flour, yeast, salt, and water are the basics. <u>Flour:</u> I recommend a good bread flour. It has more protein than all-purpose flour and will give your bread a crusty, coarse texture. If you have nothing more in the house than all-purpose, use it. You will still have a good outcome. <u>Yeast:</u> Get good fast-rise yeast such as Fleischmann's. <u>Salt:</u> Don't leave out the salt, and don't be afraid to use the amount called for in the recipe; it usually proves to be right. <u>Water:</u> Lukewarm is the best. The key here is to let the yeast and the water dissolve together until the yeast foams up, about 8 minutes.

Rising Time: Three risings make for the best bread. For example, make the bread and let it rise until doubled in size, 1½ to 2 hours. Punch the dough down and let it rise back up, about 1 hour. Lastly, punch the dough down and shape it into loaves. Let it rise a third time, until the loaves are doubled in size; about 1 hour, then bake. I have also discovered that placing a small pan filled with water below the baking bread creates steam and gives the bread a hard crust. Invest in a baking stone and always sprinkle cornmeal onto the stone before placing your shaped loaves. The stone will definitely make a difference. This is the perfect scenario for bread making, but if you work or do not have time, put the bread together before you have to leave and place it in the refrigerator covered with plastic wrap. When you get home, punch it down and shape it into loaves. Let it rise up and bake. Dinner rolls, pizza, and focaccia bread usually need only to rise once or twice. Using a food processor, or making the bread by hand is your preference; just be sure to knead the bread dough 8 to 10 minutes until it becomes elastic.

Pizza Making: Pizza making is not hard, and once you get the hang of it, you will want to make your own. Patience is the key. Rising time is not the most important thing, but waiting for the risen dough to relax before stretching is essential. In order to get the dough to the size you desire, let the dough rest in between rolling it out. The dough has to rest and rise a little before it will let you stretch it again. Have fun and make it a project with the kids. Make it thick, like *Sicilian Pizza,* or thin-crusted, and enjoy the work of your hands.

(Time: 5 Minutes)

Italian Bread Crumbs

NOTE: *Italian bread crumbs are an essential in the Italian kitchen. Don't be surprised if Italian bread crumb recipes vary from dish to dish. There are many combinations of bread crumbs, cheese, garlic, and parsley. The combinations depend on the type of breading or filling used.*

1 cup plain bread crumbs
⅓ cup grated Parmesan cheese
2 cloves garlic, minced
¼ cup fresh Italian flat-leaf parsley
1 teaspoon salt
¼ teaspoon ground black pepper

1. Mix all ingredients together. These bread crumbs can be used immediately or stored in a covered container. Use this for bread crumb filling in ground meats or toasted over casseroles.

ROSALIE TEACHING BREAD MAKING TO ALEXANDRA AND HER MOTHER, TAMI HARPOLE

Modiga
(ITALIAN TOASTED BREAD CRUMBS)

NOTE: *This garnish is wonderful on red or cream sauces, and can be used on other Italian dishes. Double for larger crowds, and keep on hand always.*

1 tablespoon olive oil
1 medium clove garlic, minced
½ cup plain bread crumbs

1. Heat oil in small pan; add minced garlic and sauté 1 minute or less until garlic is very light brown. Add bread crumbs all at once, stirring constantly until crumbs become darker in color and are "toasted," about 2 minutes. Remove from pan into small bowl. Use about 1 tablespoon of crumbs to garnish individual pasta dishes.

(Time: 4 Hours and 30 Minutes — mostly unattended)

Homemade Italian Bread

NOTE: *This wonderful bread will definitely be worth your time. Remember, making bread can conform to your schedule. Put it together early before you go to work, and put it in the refrigerator covered with plastic wrap. Punch it down when you get home, make into loaves and bake it after rising.*

6 to 6½ cups bread flour, or all-purpose

3 teaspoons salt

2 tablespoons active dry yeast

2½ cups warm water, not hot to touch

1 tablespoon olive oil

1 - 14" pizza stone

2 tablespoons yellow cornmeal

1 egg white

1 tablespoon water

sesame seeds

1. Preheat oven to 400°F. Place 6 cups flour and salt in large bowl or pan and mix together. Put yeast in warm water and stir to dissolve, letting it foam up, for 8 to 10 minutes. Make a well in the flour mixture and add a little of the yeast water with a small amount of flour, working together and setting to side of bowl. Continue until all the flour and water have been used. Bring all the dough together; dough may be sticky. Work in the remaining ½ cup flour as needed. If dough comes together firm, you will not need the additional ½ cup flour. Knead together 8 to 10 minutes, until dough feels elastic. Pour olive oil over dough, turning to coat entire surface. Place towel over dough and let rise in warm place, 1½ to 2 hours, until doubled in size.

2. Punch dough down. Let dough rise another 1 hour.

3. After the second rising, punch dough down and divide into three parts, shaping each part into loaves. Sprinkle cornmeal on stone and place loaves 2" apart. Let rise to double in size, about 1 hour.

4. Beat the egg white and 1 tablespoon of water until foamy. Brush over the top of each loaf and sprinkle with sesame seeds. Make 2 or 3 cuts across the top of each loaf with a serrated-edge knife. Have oven preheated and put bread in oven on middle grate. Place an 8" cake pan filled half with water on grate below bread or at bottom of oven to create steam during baking. This will give the bread a hard crust.

(Homemade Italian Bread . . . continue on Page 98)

(Homemade Italian Bread . . . continue from Page 97)

5. Bake bread for 30 to 35 minutes. Remove bread from oven and let cool 5 to 10 minutes. Remove from stone. Bread should sound hollow when tapped. This bread should have a hard crust and be fairly dense inside. Serve warm with olive oil or butter or try ***Herb Dip With Olive Oil*** recipe, found on page 104. Makes 3 large loaves.

ROSALIE SERVING BREAD

Italian Sausage Bread

Italian Sausage Bread

NOTE: *This finished bread roll is beautiful and can be used as the centerpiece on your table. Use it as an accompaniment to your meal or sliced thick with a salad. Either way it is delicious. You can also use it sliced for appetizers, along with **Marinara Sauce** recipe found on page 127, for dipping.*

Basic Pizza Dough recipe found on page 112

1 pound Italian sweet sausage, about 3 long links

olive oil, for frying

1 whole egg, beaten
 plus 1 egg white
½ cup grated Parmesan cheese
8 ounces mozzarella cheese, finely shredded
¼ teaspoon dried oregano
2 tablespoons fresh curly parsley, chopped

salt and pepper to taste
1 —14" pizza stone
cornmeal for dusting stone

1 egg white
1 tablespoon water
sesame seeds to sprinkle over dough

olive oil to drizzle, optional
grated Parmesan for garnish

1. Preheat oven to 350°F. Prepare pizza dough according to recipe, letting dough rise for about 1½ hours. Punch dough down and let rest for about 15 minutes before rolling out.

2. While dough is resting, remove sausage from casings and crumble into small pieces. Fry sausage in lightly oiled skillet until browned evenly. Remove to large bowl and let cool. Add the eggs, cheeses, oregano, and parsley. Using your hands, mix the sausage mixture well until it all comes together. Set aside.

3. After the dough has rested, roll out a 14" circle and lay it on your pizza stone or a large pizza pan. Spread the meat over the dough to within 1" of the edge of the circle. Salt and pepper the meat lightly. Roll the dough jelly-roll style, placing the roll seam-side down on your stone. Be sure to scatter a little cornmeal on the bottom of the stone to keep the roll from sticking.

4. Beat the egg white and water until foamy. Brush top of loaf and sprinkle with sesame seeds. Bake for 45 minutes. Slice the roll and serve hot with olive oil to drizzle and grated cheese for garnish. Serves 8 to 10.

(Time: 3 Hours and 45 Minutes)

Italian Dinner Rolls

NOTE: *These rolls are wonderful and make any meal complete. Drizzle with olive oil or butter.*

1¼ cup warm water
3 teaspoons yeast

4½ cups bread flour, or all-purpose
2 teaspoons salt
1 egg, beaten
2 tablespoons salted butter, melted

2 teaspoons olive oil for coating dough
1 – 14" pizza stone
cornmeal for dusting stone

1 egg white
1 tablespoon water
sesame seeds, optional

1. Preheat oven to 400°F. Put yeast in warm water and stir to dissolve, letting it foam up, for 8 to 10 minutes. Place the flour in a large bowl, add the salt and mix well. Make a well in the center of the flour, add the egg and melted butter. Add the yeast water, a little at a time with the flour. Work the liquid into the flour until all incorporated. Bring all the dough together into a ball and knead 8 to 10 minutes, until dough feels elastic. If the dough is sticky, add a little more flour. Pour the olive oil over the dough and turn to coat. Let rise in a warm place for 1½ to 2 hours.

2. Punch the dough down and let it rest for 15 minutes. Divide the dough into 12 pieces and shape into rolls. Dust the stone with cornmeal and place the rolls on the stone. Cover rolls and let rise another 1 hour or until doubled in size.

3. Beat the egg white with water until foamy. Brush the rolls with the egg white and sprinkle with sesame seeds, if desired. Cut across the top of each roll with a small serrated knife. Bake in hot oven 20 minutes or until golden. Makes 12 large rolls.

Olive-Rosemary Bread

NOTE: *If you like olives, you will love this bread. Omit the olives and you have a wonderful crusty bread much like the Rosemary Bread found at many Italian restaurants.*

1 tablespoon active dry yeast
2 teaspoons extra virgin olive oil
1½ cups warm water (more if needed)

1 cup Kalamata or green olives, pitted and chopped
2 tablespoons finely chopped fresh rosemary
  or 1 tablespoon dried rosemary

5 cups bread flour, or all-purpose
3 teaspoons salt

2 teaspoons olive oil
1 – 14" pizza stone
cornmeal for dusting stone.

1. Preheat oven to 400°F. Put yeast and olive oil in warm water. Stir to dissolve, letting it foam up, for 8 to 10 minutes. Drain olives, pit and chop. Add the rosemary to the olives and set aside.

2. In a large bowl, combine the flour and salt. Mix together well. Add the olive-rosemary mixture and mix thoroughly. Add the yeast water a little at a time, gathering flour into it and set to side of bowl. Continue until all the flour and water have been brought together. Gather the dough into a ball and knead 8 to 10 minutes, until dough feels elastic. Pour olive oil over bread to coat and let rise 1½ to 2 hours or until doubled in size.

3. Punch dough down and on floured board, cut dough into 2 parts. Let dough rest for 15 minutes. Dust stone with cornmeal and shape dough into 2 loaves. Place on stone and let rise another 1 hour.

4. Make 2 cuts across the top of loaves with serrated knife. Bake for 28 to 30 minutes, until bread is golden on top. Makes 2 loaves.

Rosemary

Herb Dip with Olive Oil
(DIPPING SAUCE FOR ITALIAN BREAD)

NOTE: *This dipping oil will send your guests over the top, but remember a little goes a long way. Pack the teaspoons full when measuring out the herbs. A little extra basil won't hurt. Final tip: Pass the breath mints after dinner.*

1 teaspoon fresh oregano, chopped

1 teaspoon fresh basil, chopped

1 teaspoon fresh Italian flat-leaf parsley, chopped

1 teaspoon fresh rosemary leaves, chopped

2 cloves garlic, minced

pinch of granulated garlic

⅛ teaspoon crushed red pepper flakes

2 tablespoons extra virgin olive oil

⅛ teaspoon coarse sea salt

⅛ teaspoon coarse ground black pepper

olive oil for bread plates

1. Place the oregano, basil, parsley, and rosemary in a bowl. Add the minced garlic and using a pestle, pound the herbs and garlic together. Add the granulated garlic, red pepper flakes, olive oil, and salt and pepper. Stir together to combine. To serve, place 1 to 2 tablespoons olive oil on bread plates and add ½ teaspoon herb mixture. Dip crusty Italian bread. Makes ten ½ teaspoon servings.

Seasoned Bread Crumbs
(For Baked Fish)

NOTE: *These bread crumbs keep nicely. Use your imagination for other uses.*

2 cups plain bread crumbs
4 tablespoons olive oil
¼ cup fresh Italian flat-leaf parsley, chopped
2 teaspoons grated lemon rind

1. Mix all ingredients in a bowl until the crumbs are evenly moistened with the oil. Use over white fish fillets while baking or over baked chicken. Store in refrigerator. Makes 2 cups.

Focaccia Bread

Focaccia Bread
(WITH MOZZARELLA AND TOMATOES)

NOTE: *Focaccia bread is thicker than pizza and very easy to make. Usually made with a liberal amount of oil and herbs and baked on stones. It was the forerunner of pizzas. Dimple the dough with your fingertips before baking. This is delicious and satisfying.*

1 tablespoon active dry yeast
¾ cup warm water, a little more if needed

3 cups bread flour, or all-purpose
1½ teaspoons salt
1 tablespoon olive oil

1—14" pizza stone
1 tablespoon cornmeal

2 tablespoons olive oil, divided
½ pound fresh mozzarella cheese, drained,
   patted dry, and sliced ¼" thick

10 cherry tomatoes, halved,
   or 2 to 3 fresh Roma tomatoes, sliced ¼"
   thick, about 12 slices

1 teaspoon herbes de Province
15 fresh basil leaves

coarse sea salt
freshly coarse ground black pepper to taste

1. Preheat the oven to 425°F. Dissolve the yeast in the water and let stand 8 to 10 minutes until foaming. In a large bowl, combine the flour and salt. Mix together. Add the yeast water, a little at a time, and place the small amount of moistened flour to the side of bowl. When all flour and water have been used, bring the flour together and form into a ball. Knead the dough 8 to 10 minutes, until elastic. Pour 1 tablespoon olive oil over dough, turning to coat. Place towel over dough and let rise 1½ hours.

2. Punch dough down and let rest 15 minutes. Using rolling pin, roll dough to a 12" circle. Sprinkle the pizza stone with cornmeal. Place circle of dough on stone and brush with 1 tablespoon olive oil. Dimple the dough with your fingertips. Place the sliced mozzarella on dough starting with outer circle and work in. Place the tomatoes on or near the mozzarella. Sprinkle with herbes de Provence and top with basil leaves.

3. Sprinkle lightly with coarse salt and pepper to taste. Drizzle remaining tablespoon of olive oil over bread. Bake on stone for 20 minutes or until golden. Serve extra olive at table for dipping. Serves 4 to 6.

Garlic Herbed Croutons

NOTE: *Homemade croutons are so good you will want to make them often. Omit the herbs for a milder taste or for low-fat, rub 1 clove of garlic over the bread, and bake at 300°F for 10 minutes. Cool and cut into cubes. If you choose not to use the minced garlic, but like the taste, brown 1 clove garlic in the butter/oil mixture, discard and proceed.*

2 tablespoons olive oil
2 tablespoons butter
1 clove garlic, minced
4 to 5 thick slices Italian or French bread, slightly
   old and hardened, cut into cubes
1 teaspoon herbes de Provence
coarse sea salt to taste

1. Place olive oil and butter in a large saucepan over medium-low heat and warm until butter is melted. Add the garlic and bread cubes together. Over medium heat, turn the bread cubes occasionally, until browned all over and toasted, about 2 minutes. Sprinkle the herbes de Provence over the bread cubes and salt to taste. Continue browning and toasting for 1 more minute.

2. Remove from pan and spread onto baking sheet to cool. Store in air-tight container for up to 2 weeks. Use on your favorite salads.

$\mathcal{B}$ruschetta Bread

NOTE: *Bruschetta bread is wonderful for a meal or served as an appetizer. The toppings can be as little as olive oil, cheese, and garlic or more by adding anchovies, pepperoncinis, mushrooms and salami.*

1 loaf crusty Italian or French bread
1 to 2 tablespoons olive oil
1 large clove garlic, halved

½ cup olive oil
1 tablespoon garlic, minced
½ cup packed fresh basil leaves, chopped
½ cup fresh cherry tomatoes, halved,
   or sun-dried tomatoes, or more if desired

½ cup freshly grated Parmesan cheese, more if desired
coarse sea salt to taste
coarse ground black pepper to taste

1. Preheat oven to 400°F. With large serrated knife, slice a long loaf of crusty Italian or French bread crosswise in half. Brush the cut sides lightly with olive oil, and rub the garlic clove hard across the cut sides. Place the loaves in the oven on the grate until toasted, 6 to 8 minutes. Remove loaves to a large cookie sheet.

2. Mix the olive oil, garlic, basil leaves, and tomatoes in a bowl. Spoon onto bread, covering the two halved loaves.

3. Sprinkle on the cheese and salt and pepper to your taste. The loaves can be broken into pieces and served as is or can be put back under the broiler for about 30 seconds, enough to toast the top. Serves 8.

Portobello Mushroom Panini

NOTE: *Panini sandwiches have become very popular, and are now offered on Italian-American menus. Using your own creativity, make them with a variety of vegetables and cheeses. Panini presses are easy to find and your kids will have fun making paninis.*

8 large slices crusty Italian bread
½ cup softened butter
4 large Portobello mushrooms

½ cup extra virgin olive oil
¼ cup sweet balsamic vinegar
coarse garlic salt with dried parsley added
1 cup marinated artichoke hearts, divided

8 slices provolone cheese, sliced fresh from the deli

1. Spread softened butter on one side of the 8 bread slices and set buttered-side down on a cookie sheet. Clean the mushrooms by wiping them dry or running gently under cool water quickly, then patting dry. Remove the fine gills beneath the mushrooms or leave intact.

2. Mix together the olive oil and vinegar and pour over the mushrooms in a shallow dish. Sprinkle the mushrooms liberally with the coarse garlic salt. Let sit for about 10 minutes. Remove the mushrooms and place on hot grill for about 3 minutes on each side. If grill is not available, broil in oven about 6 minutes, turning several times. Be careful not to burn. Remove when tender. Set aside.

3. Drain artichokes; place in bowl and set aside. To assemble the panini, place 1 slice of provolone cheese on 4 slices of the unbuttered bread. Next, place the grilled or broiled portobello mushroom and ¼ cup artichoke hearts; top it with another slice cheese.

4. Top each of the panini with the remaining 4 non-buttered sides of bread. Place the panini on a grill, or in large frying pan and with a brick covered with aluminum foil. Press down on the paninis until the bread is toasted. If you have a panini press, omit the pan-fry procedure. Turn the panini over and press down again until the panini is toasted and the cheese is melted. Makes 4 paninis.

Basic Pizza Dough

NOTE: *Making your own pizzas is fun and easy, it only takes practice and patience. Use your favorite ready-to-use pizza sauce or **Marinara Sauce** recipe found on page 127. This recipe makes enough dough for two 12" Sicilian pizzas (1" thick) or six 8" (about ⅓" thick) pizzas.*

2 — 14" pizza stones
  or 6 — 8" round pans
2 teaspoons active dry yeast
1¼ cups warm water

3 cups bread flour, or all-purpose, a little more if needed
1½ teaspoons salt
2 teaspoons olive oil
1 to 2 tablespoons cornmeal

1. Preheat oven to 475°F. Put yeast in warm water, and stir to dissolve, letting it foam up for 8 to 10 minutes. Mix the flour and salt together in large bowl. Add the yeast water a little at a time with small amounts of flour. Set to the side of bowl. Continue until all the water and flour have been used. Bring the flour together and form dough into a ball. Knead the dough 8 to 10 minutes, until soft and elastic. Pour 1 teaspoon olive oil over dough, turning to coat. Cover with towel and let rise 1½ hours.

2. Punch dough down and let rest 15 minutes.

3. On floured counter, roll the dough portions a little at a time, letting the dough rest before proceeding. Pizza dough can be stretched a little at a time without leaving holes in the dough, if the dough can rest in intervals.

4. Place the pizza on the stone, and continue to roll or stretch until the circle is to the edge of the stone. Place cornmeal below the pizza dough and cover pizzas with your favorite toppings, being careful not to make the pizza too wet or too dry.

5. Bake for about 20 minutes, for one thick Sicilian pizza, or 15 to 18 minutes if cooking thinner pizzas. The pizza should be golden brown underneath and the cheeses melted on top.

Grandchildren— Reagan and Alexandra Harpole

*R*osalie's Sicilian Pizza

NOTE: *These pizzas should be about 1" thick or thicker, if desired. They taste great and the time invested is certainty worth it.*

Basic Pizza Dough recipe found on page 112

2 - 14" pizza stone

2 tablespoons cornmeal, divided

2 tablespoons olive oil, divided

2½ cups marinara or pizza sauce of your choice, divided

1 cup grated Parmesan cheese, divided

2 cups partially cooked Italian sausage, lightly browned, divided

1 cup sliced mushrooms, divided

½ cup fresh basil leaves, chopped, divided

1 cup shredded mozzarella, divided

2 tablespoons olive oil, divided

crushed red pepper flakes (optional)

1. Preheat oven to 475°F. Prepare pizza dough and punch down after rising. Let dough rest 15 minutes. Divide dough into 2 parts.

2. Place 1 part of the dough on a lightly floured board. Using rolling pin, roll the dough into a 12" circle, letting the dough rest in intervals before continuing to roll out completely. Sprinkle pizza stone with 1 tablespoon of cornmeal and transfer dough to pizza stone. Make a raised ridge all around the edge of the dough.

3. Working with 1 pizza at a time, brush the dough with 1 tablespoon olive oil. Add 1¼ cups marinara sauce, ½ cup Parmesan cheese, 1 cup Italian crumbled sausage, ½ cup mushroom slices, ¼ cup fresh basil leaves, and ½ cup mozzarella. Drizzle 1 tablespoon olive oil over the pizza. Garnish by sprinkling with crushed red pepper flakes, if desired. Set completed pizza aside and allow to rise a little more.

4. Prepare the second pizza, using the remaining ingredients or add pepperoni instead of sausage, and olives instead of mushrooms.

5. Bake the pizzas for about 20 minutes. Pizza should be browned on the bottom and bubbly on top.

All About Pasta

Pasta is one of the most popular foods in the world. Composed mainly of starch and protein, it is low in calories and good for us. A plate of pasta can be made as simply as putting a little olive oil and basil on top, and garnished with Parmesan cheese. Or, it can be quite glorious, with creamy Alfredo sauce cooked up with shrimp and crabmeat. In any case, there are some things to remember when cooking pasta. Note the six rules below:

Rule 1: Always use a good brand, one made with 100% durum wheat with semolina as the first ingredient listed. Like anything, use the best for the best results.

Rule 2: Always use plenty of water, usually an 8-quart pot with 5 to 6 quarts of water to boil 1 pound of pasta. Add salt, at least 1 tablespoon per pound; most Italian authorities use 1 tablespoon per 3 quarts water. I usually go with 1 heaping tablespoon per pot of water. Do not use oil in the water. Italians do not use it.

Rule 3: Keep the water boiling, and stir often to avoid sticking. Do Not Overcook! Taste the pasta and always take if off a little early. It will continue cooking from sauce to table. It should have a little bite, thus the saying *al dente*, meaning "firm to the bite" or "until done."

Rule 4: Don't over drain and never "rinse." In fact, I like to use a spaghetti spoon and lift the pasta right out of the water and into the sauce while the sauce is still hot, letting the two simmer together for just a minute. The pasta will absorb some of the sauce and the sauce will intensify in flavor. Letting some of the pasta water cling to the pasta causes the starch to adhere to the sauce. If you do use a colander, drain quickly and then put in your pasta bowl. Reserving pasta water to thin the sauce a little is used by every Italian cook.

Rule 5: Pasta cools quickly, so serve it as soon as possible for the best results. Warming your large pasta bowl in the oven for a few minutes is also helpful. Have your garnishes at the table: extra olive oil to drizzle, freshly grated cheese, and freshly ground course black pepper are musts. Use the recipe for ***Modiga***, found on page 95, which is Italian toasted bread crumbs, to send your guests over the top. Investing in a cheese grater and pepper grinder will more than pay for themselves in enjoyment.

Rule 6: Freshly made pasta is truly a "must do" once in your lifetime. Invest in a pasta machine, and have a lot of fun with your family. However, I like to make ravioli by hand. Fresh pasta almost melts in your mouth and cooks much faster than dried. This is an eating experience to be cherished.

Beautify

the Table

Entertaining
Family, Friends, and Special Guests

Hotel Hospitality: Growing up in a typical Italian family afforded me the opportunity to witness what I call "Hotel Hospitality." My mother and dad loved to have company, and I can honestly say there was no respecter of persons. It didn't matter if they were family, friends, special guests or total strangers; the "red carpet" was always rolled out. It wasn't the elaborate home or the finery of decor the people enjoyed, but rather the warmth of the hospitality they loved. The fact that everyone that came by was treated "royally" was one of the magnets that drew people from everywhere. My mother always had stored tins of Italian cookies in her pantry and even if you just knocked on the door to deliver a package, she would invite you in, make you sit down and serve you a cookie and drink. Whether it was just a small group of her auxiliary ladies from church, or an important family event, everyone was treated the same. All would come away feeling loved, fed, and truly entertained. These lessons have been invaluable to me. Being the wife of a minister for many years, I have had the opportunity to entertain people from all walks of life in my home. Just as my mother put the excitement of preparing meals for guests into me, so did I instill this into my own children.

Tried and True: When entertaining special guests, serve a meal that you feel confident preparing. One that received previous praises from your own family is usually safe. Believe me, this will cut your stress in half.

Set the Table: Give your guests a dining experience they will never forget. Not only should they remember the wonderful food, but they should never forget the beautiful table. Use your best dishes, tableware and glasses. If you don't have napkins to match, consider using nice, large paper ones. I love to use napkin rings and place the ringed napkins on my empty soup or salad plates. Napkin rings can be very costly, so do as I do and buy silk flower bunches. Take them off individually, curl the wire ends into a small circle, and use them as beautiful napkin rings. And never forsake the garage sales. You can find many wonderful table decorations very reasonable. I have purchased sets of brand-new dishes, candle arrangements, sets of beautiful glasses, and an array of fine dinning accessories at very affordable prices.

Candles and Flowers: Lit candles bring warmth and serenity to the table. They are very inexpensive, and can be as simple as a few floating in a bowl or elegant stems in holders. A vase of flowers is also nice, especially in summer when they are in full bloom. Cut a few from your garden, or pick up a bundle at the grocer. Your guests will love them.

Dessert for Everyone: Don't forget dessert. Even if your guests say they are full and don't have room, while lingering at the table they will usually change their mind. Desserts can usually be made the day before and stored either on the shelf or in the refrigerator. Remember, nothing tops off a wonderful meal like a wonderful dessert. If they don't remember the meal, (which they will of course), they will remember the dessert, and tell you about it years later.

Treat Family Royally: As much as I love to entertain others, I must say nothing gives me more joy than to serve my family. Every tip that I have given you above first applies to my family. I can remember a particular time when my children were young. It had been a crazy week, running to piano lessons with Scott, Junior Camp coming up for Jeff, and sleepovers for Dana and her friends. In the middle of all the week's activities, I noticed that there was one night for all of us to be together. I got the idea to make it a memorable one. I had frozen some extra Red Sauce with Meat, so I decided to serve their favorite, Penne Pasta with Red Sauce. The salad was easy to make and that gave me time to make the dessert. I only had an hour until everyone would be home, but I managed to set a gorgeous table using our best china complete with a vase of roses from our yard. When everyone came in they looked around in amazement and asked: 'Who in the world is coming for dinner"? I looked at them and said, "Why, all of you, of course". That night we not only ate the wonderful Italian food, but we talked, laughed and truly enjoyed each other. It was a memory that all of us cherished. I can honestly say I did that often and made sure that the ones closest to me knew they were still first in my life. So let me encourage you to sit down with your family, even if there are only two of you. Have some fun, set the table and treat each other royally.

Italian Peppermint Sauce

NOTE: *This sauce is delicious on grilled breaded meat, such as spiedini, steak, or grilled chicken, and some baked fish. Use a large bunch of peppermint sprigs to swathe the sauce on your meat. You may want to grow your own peppermint, as you will use this sauce often.*

¼ cup fresh peppermint leaves, packed

1 large clove garlic, chopped

1 large fresh tomato, cored, peeled and chopped fine, about 1 cup
  or ½ cup diced tomatoes, juice included

¼ cup extra virgin olive oil

1 to 2 teaspoons fresh lemon juice

2 tablespoons water

½ teaspoon coarse sea salt, more for your taste

1. Place peppermint and chopped garlic in a wooden bowl and pound with a wooden pestle until smashed together, about 1 minute. Remove to larger bowl and add the chopped tomato. Add the olive oil, lemon juice, water, and salt. Stir together. This recipe can be easily doubled if you have a large amount of meat to garnish. In the winter, use canned style diced tomatoes. It makes about 1 cup per recipe.

Garlic Butter Sauce

NOTE: *This sauce has so many uses. Add various herbs, such as fresh chopped parsley, herbes de Provence, or crushed red pepper, for an additional boost.*

1 stick salted butter
2 teaspoons minced garlic
2 teaspoons fresh squeezed lemon juice, or more if desired
coarse sea salt to taste
ground pepper to taste

1. Sauté the minced garlic in 2 tablespoons butter over medium heat for 1 to 2 minutes, until garlic becomes slightly golden. Add the remaining butter, and warm until melted. Add the lemon juice, and salt and pepper to taste. This recipe will make about ½ cup sauce. Use on broiled or grilled fish and meats, or on some vegetables, such as boiled or baked potatoes.

Rosalie's Red Sauce
(WITH MEAT #1)

NOTE: *Try the Italian toasted bread crumbs to top off this traditional dish for an extra boost. We call it "Modiga." This is one of my favorite red sauces and has been in my family for three generations.*

1 pound penne pasta or spaghetti

¼ cup olive oil

1 small onion (about ½ cup)

1 (15-ounce) can whole tomatoes, juice
   included

3 teaspoons sugar

1 teaspoon dried basil leaves

½ teaspoon salt

¼ teaspoon ground black pepper

1¼ cups homemade or low-sodium canned
   chicken broth

1 (29-ounce) can tomato sauce

2 (6-ounce) cans tomato paste

1 large chicken breast with rib bone

coarse garlic salt with dried parsley

olive oil for frying

2 Italian sausage links

1 pound pork rib tips, cut into 4" pieces,
   or 3 to 4 pork neck bones

Italian Meatballs recipe found on page 125

freshly ground coarse black pepper

freshly grated Parmesan cheese for garnish

Modiga (Italian Toasted Bread Crumbs)

recipe found on page 95

1. In an 8-quart heavy pot, sauté onion in olive oil until translucent and slightly brown, about 2 minutes. Remove from heat.

2. Pour whole tomatoes into a large bowl. Remove hard stems or any unsightly pieces and discard. Chop tomatoes fine and add to onion. Return to heat and bring tomatoes to soft boil. Add the sugar, basil, salt, pepper, and chicken broth. Cook over medium heat, 6 to 8 minutes. Add tomato sauce, rinsing can with a little water, and add to sauce. Add tomato paste and stir. Cover and simmer on very low heat.

3. Prepare meat. Rinse chicken breast in cold water and pat dry. Sprinkle breast with garlic salt on both sides. Fry in olive oil 6 to 8 minutes on each side. While chicken is browning, add the sausage and rib tips to the pan and brown. When all browned, add to the sauce.

4. Prepare Italian meatballs, then brown lightly in olive oil, and add to sauce. It will appear that this is too much meat for the sauce, but it will all cook together and the sauce will thin out. Bring sauce and meat to gentle boil, stirring often to prevent sticking. Reduce heat to gentle simmer, cover, and cook 1 hour.

5. When sauce is completed, remove chicken and sausage. Cut in medium pieces, and return to sauce or along with rib tips, serve in bowl on table. Skim any oil from top of sauce and discard. This is a thick, meaty sauce.

6. Boil pasta al dente, according to package directions. Drain quickly so pasta will not be dry. Add to the sauce. Garnish with freshly ground coarse black pepper and freshly grated Parmesan cheese. Add Italian toasted bread crumbs on top, if desired. Serve with Italian salad and crusty hot bread. Serves 4 to 6.

ROSALIE SERVING HER FAMILY

Red Sauce over Penne

Italian Meatballs
(FOR ROSALIE'S RED SAUCE WITH MEAT)

NOTE: *These meatballs are wonderful, and can also be used in a variety of soups and sauces, or made into patties for Italian Hamburgers.*

1½ pounds lean ground beef

2 to 3 cloves garlic, chopped

½ cup plain bread crumbs

⅓ cup grated Parmesan cheese

3 eggs

3 tablespoons fresh curly parsley, chopped
  or 2 teaspoons dried parsley

1 teaspoon fennel seed

1½ teaspoons salt

¼ teaspoon ground black pepper

olive oil for frying

1. Mix all ingredients in a large bowl and form into 2" round balls. In skillet with olive oil, lightly brown meatballs on all sides. Do not cook to completion. Add the meatballs to the sauce and continue to cook until the sauce and other added meats are done, usually about 1 hour. This makes about 36 meatballs.

Rosalie's Red Sauce
(WITH MEAT #2, FOR A LARGE CROWD)

NOTE: *This recipe makes a large pot of sauce, plenty for a large crowd and enough left over to freeze. Use heavy gallon freezer bags and enjoy anytime. Be sure to use 2 large pots to boil 1 pound of pasta in each.*

2 pounds penne pasta or spaghetti of your choice

¼ cup olive oil
1 medium onion, chopped, about ⅔ cup

1 (32-ounce) can whole tomatoes, with juice
4 teaspoons sugar
1½ teaspoons dried basil leaves
½ teaspoon ground black pepper
1½ cups homemade or canned low-sodium chicken broth
2 (29-ounce) cans tomato sauce plus 1 (15-ounce) can tomato sauce
3 (6-ounce) cans tomato paste

2 chicken breasts with rib bone
2 links Italian sausage
4 to 5 pork neck bones,
    or 2 to 3 rib tips or country style ribs

Italian Meatballs recipe, doubled, found on page 125
freshly grated Parmesan cheese
Modiga (Italian Toasted Bread Crumbs) recipe found on page 95
freshly ground coarse black pepper

1. Prepare above recipe the same as you would for ***Rosalie's Red Sauce With Meat #1*** recipe found on pages 122 and 123. This sauce will be thick and meaty. If needed, add a little additional chicken broth. Garnish with freshly grated Parmesan cheese, Italian toasted bread crumbs, and freshly ground coarse black pepper. Serves 10 to 15.

Marinara Sauce

NOTE: *This sauce can be stored in refrigerator for 1 to 2 days or frozen in zipper bags. Use over pasta, in vegetable dishes, as a dip for appetizers, or in meatless lasagna. Variation: Add **Italian Meatballs** recipe found on page 125, for a quick meat sauce.*

¼ cup olive oil
1 small onion, chopped
2 cloves garlic, chopped

1 (15-ounce) can whole tomatoes, juice included
2 teaspoons sugar
½ teaspoon dried basil leaves
½ cup homemade or low-sodium canned chicken broth
⅛ teaspoon crushed red pepper flakes
½ teaspoon salt
¼ teaspoon ground black pepper

1 (15-ounce) can tomato sauce
4 to 5 tablespoons tomato paste, for thickening
few parsley leaves

1. Pour olive oil in large saucepan and sauté onions and garlic about 2 minutes, until lightly golden.

2. Pour tomatoes in bowl, removing any hard stems or unsightly pieces and discard. Chop tomatoes fine and add to onion/garlic mixture. Over medium heat begin to simmer sauce. Add the sugar, dried basil leaves, chicken broth, crushed red pepper flakes, and salt and pepper. Continue to simmer 5 to 6 minutes.

3. Add the tomato sauce, paste, and a few parsley leaves. With the lid on, turn the heat to low and simmer about 15 minutes. Stir often to avoid scorching on bottom. If sauce is too thick, add 1 to 2 tablespoons of water. Taste sauce and add more seasoning, if desired. Makes 4 cups.

Sausage & Pepper Sauce
(WITH ROTINI)

NOTE: *If you like peppers and sausage, you'll love this dish. Dip the Italian bread in the sauce for an extra treat.*

1 pound rotini
1 tablespoon salt
½ cup reserved pasta water

3 peppers; green, red, yellow, or mixed
¼ cup olive oil
1 small onion, chopped, about ½ cup
2 cloves garlic, chopped
salt and pepper to taste
2 Italian sausage links cut into 2" rounds

1 (15-ounce) can tomato sauce
½ teaspoon sugar, or more if desired
¼ teaspoon dried basil leaves
¼ teaspoon crushed red pepper flakes
¼ cup homemade or low-sodium canned chicken broth
salt and pepper to taste

freshly grated Parmesan cheese
olive oil

1. Wash, core, and seed peppers. Cut in julienne pieces, not too thin. Place peppers in saucepan with olive oil, onion, and garlic. Salt and pepper to taste. Add sausage and sauté until peppers are tender and sausage is cooked.

2. Add tomato sauce, sugar, basil, crushed red pepper flakes, chicken broth, and salt and pepper to taste. Simmer sauce on low heat, about 15 minutes.

3. Boil rotini in an 8-quart pot boiling water with 1 tablespoon salt added. Cook al dente and drain. Toss together with sauce. Add reserved pasta water.

4. Serve garnished with grated Parmesan cheese and additional olive oil at the table, if desired. Serves 4 to 6.

(Time: 2 Hours and 45 Minutes)

Baked Lasagna

NOTE: *An ever-popular Italian dish, lasagna is perfect for Sunday dinner. Make it on Saturday, cover and put in the refrigerator. Pop it in the oven the next day and you have very little work. Serve with Italian salad and hot bread and you'll have rave reviews. To top this off serve with* **Italian Lemon Ice** *recipe found on page 227.*

Red Sauce with Meat #1 recipe found
  on pages 122 and 123

1 pound lasagna
1 tablespoon salt
lasagna pan 10" x 15" x 3"

2 pounds ricotta cheese, about 4 cups
2 tablespoons fresh Italian flat-leaf parsley,
  chopped or 2 teaspoons, dried

1 cup grated Parmesan cheese
2 eggs
salt and pepper to taste

1 (16-ounce) bag shredded mozzarella cheese
½ cup freshly grated Parmesan cheese

1. Preheat oven to 350°F. Prepare the sauce according to recipe, crumbling the hamburger, instead of making meatballs. Remove other meat, such as chicken, sausage, or pork. Cut into small pieces and put back into sauce. If this is too much meat, serve in bowl on table for additional serving.

2. Boil the lasagna in an 8-quart pot boiling water with 1 tablespoon salt added. Undercook lasagna 3 to 4 minutes to accommodate for baking time. Drain and put back in pot with lukewarm water to keep lasagna noodles from sticking as you work with them.

3. Place ricotta, parsley, cheese, and eggs in bowl and mix well. Add salt and pepper to taste.

4. In large lasagna pan, cover bottom with thin layer of sauce. Add a layer of lasagna strips (about 3) and place teaspoons of the ricotta filling over strips. Sprinkle some shredded mozzarella over ricotta. Add sauce with meat, crumbling any large clumps of meat. Repeat layers, using the lasagna, ricotta, mozzarella, and sauce. Stop about 1/2 inch from top of pan to avoid spilling over in oven. On last layer, omit ricotta. Pour sauce over entire area and garnish with remaining mozzarella and the grated cheese.

5. Cover with foil, piercing a few places with knife for steam to escape. Bake in oven for 35 to 40 minutes. Lasagna is done when bubbly and heated through. Serves 8 to 10.

Stuffed Jumbo Shells

NOTE: *These stuffed shells are absolutely wonderful. Served with Italian salad and bread, it makes for a great dinner menu.*

Marinara Sauce recipe found on page 127
Italian Meatballs recipe found on page 125, optional

½ package jumbo shells, about 18
1 tablespoon salt
13" x 9" x 2" glass baking dish
olive oil to brush pan

1 (15-ounce) container ricotta cheese
1½ cups shredded mozzarella cheese
½ cup grated Pecorino Romano cheese
1 egg, beaten
2 tablespoons fresh Italian flat-leaf parsley, chopped

½ cup shredded mozzarella cheese
½ cup Parmesan cheese

1. Preheat oven to 350 °F. Prepare the marinara sauce. If using the Italian meatballs, brown, crumble, and add to sauce. Simmer together about 15 minutes. Boil jumbo shells in 6-quart pot with 4 quarts boiling water. Add 1 tablespoon salt and boil 8 to 10 minutes. Shells should be a little undercooked, to accommodate baking time.

2. While shells are cooking, mix together ricotta, mozzarella, Pecorino Romano, egg, and parsley.

3. Drain shells and cover with lukewarm water to keep separated. Remove 1 shell at a time and stuff with ricotta mixture. Lightly brush bottom of baking dish with olive oil. Place 1 cup marinara sauce over bottom of dish and arrange filled shells on top of sauce. Pour 2 cups additional sauce over shells.

4. Top with ½ cup mozzarella and ½ cup Parmesan cheese. Cover with foil, making a few slits in foil for steam to escape. Bake 30 minutes, until hot and bubbly. Let stand 6 to 8 minutes before serving. Serves 6.

Stuffed Jumbo Shells

Classic Fettuccine Alfredo

NOTE: *This is a classic recipe. The sauce is often made right at the table in some elite Italian restaurants. This pasta is best when eaten immediately after cooking.*

1 pound fettuccine
1 tablespoon salt
reserved pasta water, if needed

2 tablespoons butter
2 eggs
I cup heavy whipping cream, room temperature
I cup Parmesan cheese
salt to taste
fine ground black pepper to taste

freshly ground coarse black pepper
freshly grated Parmesan cheese

1. Boil fettuccine in an 8-quart pot boiling water with 1 tablespoon salt added.

2. While fettuccine is cooking, warm a large pasta bowl in the oven, 350°F., for about 5 minutes. Warm the butter in a small saucepan on very low heat, about 5 minutes, until the butter turns golden. Be careful not to burn. Crack the eggs into the warm bowl and immediately start beating eggs. Add the cream and beat into eggs. The cream and eggs will become thick. Add the cheese and continue to stir together. Add the butter and salt and pepper to taste.

3. When fettuccine is cooked *al dente*, using a spaghetti spoon, lift the pasta right out of the water and into the pasta bowl. Toss together. Use a little reserved pasta water if fettuccine appears too dry.

4. Garnish with freshly ground coarse black pepper. Pass extra Parmesan cheese at the table. Serves 4 to 6.

Rosalie's Fettuccine Alfredo

NOTE: *This is an all-time favorite, and so easy to make. The sauce will seem like too much at first, but the pasta will take it up. The Modiga garnish really enhances this dish.*

1 pound fettuccine
1 tablespoon salt

4 tablespoons unsalted butter
1 tablespoon olive oil
3 cloves garlic, minced
4 cups heavy whipping cream, room temperature

4 cups grated Parmesan cheese
1 ounce Velveeta cheese, (regular, not light)
1 tablespoon fresh Italian flat-leaf parsley, chopped
salt and fine ground black pepper to taste

freshly ground coarse black pepper
Modiga (Italian Toasted Bread Crumbs) recipe found on page 95

1. Boil fettuccine in an 8-quart pot boiling water with 1 tablespoon salt added.

2. While fettuccine is cooking, melt butter with olive oil over low heat. Add garlic and heat together gently, about 1 minute. Add cream and continue to stir until heated through.

3. Add the grated Parmesan, 1 cup at a time, stirring slowly into the sauce. Add the Velveeta cheese, parsley, and salt and pepper to taste. Stir gently until cheeses are fully melted and blended together. Keep the sauce on very low heat or remove, as sauce can burn easily.

4. When fettuccine is cooked al dente, using spaghetti spoon, lift pasta right out of water and put it directly into saucepan with sauce. Toss and let heat together about 1 minute. Transfer fettuccine to large platter. Garnish with freshly ground coarse black pepper and Italian toasted bread crumbs. Serves 6.

Pasta with Fresh Tomatoes & Basil

NOTE: *The secrets to this dish are the fresh ingredients and serving it as soon as it is done. This is a classic Italian fresh tomato sauce, light and full of flavor. It is easy to become addicted. This dish deserves lots of freshly grated Parmesan cheese.*

1 pound angel hair, vermicelli, or linguine pasta
1 tablespoon salt
½ to 1 cup reserved pasta water

2 large vine-ripened tomatoes, cored and chopped, about 2 cups
½ cup extra virgin olive oil
1 tablespoon garlic, minced
½ cup fresh basil leaves, tightly packed and shredded
1 teaspoon coarse sea salt, or more for taste
¼ teaspoon freshly ground coarse black pepper, or more for taste

freshly grated Parmesan cheese for garnish.
Crushed red pepper flakes for garnish (optional)

1. Use large, fresh, firm tomatoes from the garden. Dip tomatoes in boiling water 1 minute to make peelings come off easily or use unpeeled if desired. Cut tomatoes in small chunks and place with juice in large pasta bowl. Add the olive oil, minced garlic, fresh basil leaves, and salt and pepper. Mix together lightly.

2. Boil pasta in an 8-quart pot of boiling water with 1 tablespoon salt added. If using angel hair, only boil about 3 to 4 minutes. Using spaghetti spoon, remove pasta right out of water into pasta bowl with tomato mixture.

3. Toss together, adding reserved pasta water if pasta gets too dry. Serve immediately garnished with freshly grated Parmesan cheese and red pepper flakes, if desired. Serves 4 to 6.

Cheese with Grater

Rosalie's Pasta con Broccoli

NOTE: *I must admit to putting an American touch on this dish by using the Velveeta. I used it once to thicken the sauce a little and loved it so much that I made it part of the recipe. This dish could be one of the most popular in the Italian-American cuisine.*

1 pound medium shell pasta

1 tablespoon salt

¼ stick butter

¼ cup olive oil

3 cloves garlic, chopped fine

3 cups broccoli florets

2 cups white capped mushrooms, sliced thick

1 teaspoon coarse sea salt

¼ teaspoon coarse ground black pepper

4 cups heavy whipping cream

4 cups grated Parmesan cheese

1 ounce Velveeta cheese (regular, not light)

freshly ground coarse black pepper, as desired

Modiga (Italian Toasted Bread Crumbs) recipe found on page 95

1. Boil shells in an 8-quart pot boiling water with 1 tablespoon salt added.

2. While shells are cooking, melt butter and olive oil in a 4-quart saucepan. Add garlic, broccoli, mushrooms, and salt and pepper. Stir-fry over medium heat 5 to 6 minutes for crisp-tender vegetables. Add cream and continue to stir until heated through. Add the cheese 1 cup at a time, stirring slowly, until the cheese is fully melted into the cream. Add the Velveeta and stir in gently until fully melted. Keep heat on low and stir often, being careful not to burn, or remove from heat completely.

3. When shells are cooked *al dente,* drain quickly, and place in a large warmed pasta bowl or platter. Pour the sauce over the shells. Toss together well. Garnish with additional freshly ground coarse black pepper and Italian toasted bread crumbs if desired. Serves 6.

Angel Hair con Broccoli

NOTE: *This dish is very light and nourishing, since all of the water from cooking the broccoli stays in the dish. At first, it will seem like too much juice, but the pasta will take it up. The simplicity of the flavors makes this a refreshing change.*

6 ounces angel hair pasta
6 cups water
2 teaspoons salt

4 cups fresh broccoli florets
¼ cup olive oil
coarse sea salt to taste
coarse ground black pepper to taste

grated Parmesan cheese for garnish, if desired

1. In a 3-quart pot, bring water and salt to boiling. Add the broccoli florets and boil for 3 to 4 minutes, until barely tender. Add the angel hair pasta and cook together with the broccoli for an additional 3 to 4 minutes. Take the pot off the stove, add the olive oil and salt and pepper to taste. Stir together. Do not drain any of the juice. Dip by ladle into individual pasta bowls, adding a little of the juice to each bowl.

2. Garnish with Parmesan cheese. Serves 4.

Pasta with Cauliflower
(QUICK PASTA)

NOTE: *This is a delightful dish, one that my entire family enjoys. My mother would make it when she needed something quick, thus the name, Quick Pasta.*

1 (12-ounce) package angel hair or vermicelli pasta
1 tablespoon salt
1 cup or more reserved pasta water, if needed

¼ cup olive oil
1 small onion, chopped, about 1/4 cup
2 cloves garlic, chopped
2 cups raw cauliflower florets
½ teaspoon salt
⅛ teaspoon ground black pepper

2 fresh tomatoes, peeled, cored and quartered,
   or 1 (15-ounce) can diced tomatoes, juice included
5 to 6 fresh basil leaves, chopped,
   or ½ teaspoon dried basil leaves
1 teaspoon sugar
salt and pepper to taste
1 tablespoon olive oil

freshly grated Parmesan cheese
freshly ground coarse black pepper to taste

1. Stir-fry onion, garlic, and cauliflower in olive oil over medium heat until crisp-tender, 10 to 12 minutes. Salt and pepper the vegetables while frying. Add tomatoes, basil, sugar, and salt and pepper to cauliflower mixture. Simmer together about 8 minutes on low heat.

2. Boil pasta in an 8-quart pot of boiling water with 1 tablespoon salt added. Do not overcook. Drain pasta, reserve at least 1 cup pasta water; use more if pasta seems dry. Add pasta to sauce with 1 tablespoon olive oil and toss together well. Pour pasta in large pasta bowl and garnish with freshly grated cheese and freshly ground coarse black pepper. Serves 4.

Pasta Primavera

NOTE: *Variation: Try this with ½ cup heavy whipping cream in addition to the red sauce. If using cream, bring to room temperature, and omit reserved pasta water. This dish is great when the summer vegetables are in; however, it can be made with whatever you have on hand.*

1 pound rigatoni or 12 ounces spaghetti

1 tablespoon salt

½ cup reserved pasta water

⅓ cup olive oil, more if needed for frying

1 small onion, chopped

3 cloves garlic, chopped

1 small zucchini, unpeeled, sliced into ¼"
   rounds, about 1 cup

1 large bell pepper, yellow or red,
   sliced into strips

⅔ cup cauliflower florets

⅔ cup broccoli florets (optional)

½ cup asparagus spears, hard stems trimmed,
   cut into thirds

salt

1 (15-ounce) can tomato sauce

½ teaspoon sugar

½ teaspoon dried basil

salt and pepper to taste

½ cup cherry tomatoes, halved

1 tablespoon olive oil

freshly grated Parmesan cheese

freshly ground coarse black pepper

1. Pour olive oil into a 4-quart heavy saucepan. Add the onion, garlic, zucchini, bell pepper, cauliflower, broccoli, and asparagus. Stir-fry the vegetables over medium heat, until crisp-tender, 8 to10 minutes. Salt the vegetables lightly while frying.

2. Add tomato sauce, sugar, basil, and salt and pepper. Cook 5 minutes longer. Add cherry tomatoes and put mixture on very low heat, just enough to keep warm.

3. Boil pasta in an 8-quart pot boiling water with 1 tablespoon salt added. Cook al dente. Be careful not to overcook. Drain all but about ½ cup pasta water.

4. Add olive oil. Toss together with the vegetables and top with generous amount of cheese and freshly ground coarse black pepper. Serves 6 to 8.

Rosalie's Angel Hair Florentine

NOTE: *You'll love how pretty this dish looks on your table. Serve it in a large pasta platter, garnished with parsley leaves during the holidays or any time. I call this dish "Christmas Pasta" because of the colors red, white, and green. Serve with Italian crusty bread and get ready for the praise.*

1 (12-once) package angel hair pasta

1 tablespoon salt

1 cup reserved pasta water, more if needed

2 skinless chicken breasts

coarse ground garlic salt with parsley

1 cup olive oil, divided

5 to 6 cloves garlic, chopped fine

¾ cup extra virgin olive oil

1 (9-ounce) bag fresh spinach leaves,
   cleaned and air-dried

1 cup grape tomatoes

salt and ground black pepper to taste

1 cup freshly grated Parmesan cheese

freshly ground coarse black pepper

extra olive for garnish

1. Rinse chicken breasts in cold water, pat dry, and cut away any fat or gristle. Sprinkle both sides liberally with the coarse garlic salt and sauté in ¼ cup olive oil 10 to 12 minutes turning occasionally, until done. Put lid on chicken and steam for 2 minutes longer. Cool, cut into small strips, and set aside.

2. Add chopped garlic to remaining ¾ cup olive oil and place in large saucepan, enough to hold both sauce and pasta. Heat gently, about 1 minute. Add spinach, tomatoes, and chicken. Stir together, until heated through, about 3 minutes.

3. Boil pasta in an 8-quart pot boiling water with 1 tablespoon salt added. Cook angel hair 3 to 4 minutes. Do not overcook. Using a spaghetti spoon, lift pasta right out of the water and place it in the pan with the sauce. Add 1 cup or a little more reserved pasta water.

4. Stir pasta with spinach/chicken mixture, until well coated together. Add salt and ground black pepper to taste.

5. Transfer to large pasta platter. Garnish with freshly grated Parmesan cheese and some freshly ground coarse black pepper. Provide extra olive oil at table, if desired. Serve the pasta at once for full flavor and to avoid getting dry. Serves 4-6.

Vermicelli with Peas and Pancetta

Vermicelli with Peas & Pancetta

NOTE: *This is a delightful dish, with the ricotta and cheese coating the vermicelli for a creamy effect. The frozen fresh peas are crunchy and along with the pancetta and mushrooms, there is plenty of flavor. If you do not have pancetta on hand, thick-sliced bacon can be used.*

1 pound vermicelli
1 tablespoon salt

4 slices pancetta, cut into strips
4 tablespoons olive oil, divided
1 medium onion, chopped fine, about 1 cup
1 cup thick sliced white mushrooms

1 (10-once) package frozen peas
1 cup reserved pasta water

1 (15-ounce) carton ricotta cheese
1 cup freshly grated Pecorino Romano cheese
1 teaspoon coarse sea salt
½ teaspoon coarse ground black pepper

crushed red pepper flakes to garnish
freshly grated Parmesan cheese for garnish

1. Fry pancetta in 2 tablespoons olive oil until crisp. Remove, chop into 1" pieces, and place in large pasta bowl. Add another tablespoon olive oil to pan and sauté onion until lightly browned, about 6 to 8 minutes. Remove and add to pancetta. With remaining 1 tablespoon olive oil, sauté mushrooms until browned, 3 to 4 minutes. Add to pancetta and onions.

2. Boil vermicelli in an 8-quart pot boiling water with 1 tablespoon salt added, for 6 to 8 minutes. During last 2 minutes of cooking time, add peas. Reserve 1 cup pasta water and drain pasta and peas together. Add to pasta bowl, containing pancetta, onions, and mushrooms. Add the 1 cup reserved pasta water and toss together.

3. Add the ricotta, grated Pecorino Romano, and salt and pepper. Toss again until all the pasta is coated with the ricotta and cheese. Garnish top with crushed red pepper flakes and freshly grated Parmesan cheese. Serves 8.

Basil Pesto Sauce
(OVER LINGUINE)

NOTE: *A classic Italian sauce. Grow sweet basil in your garden all summer and freeze pesto sauce for winter use, adding a little extra olive oil. It is best to freeze without the cheese and add it when ready to use.*

1 pound linguine
1 tablespoon salt
½ cup reserved pasta water, more if needed

2 cups fresh basil leaves
2 tablespoons pignoli (pine nuts)
3 to 4 cloves garlic, chopped
1 cup extra virgin olive oil

½ cup freshly grated Parmesan cheese
¼ teaspoon coarse sea salt
coarse ground black pepper to taste
freshly grated Parmesan cheese for garnish

1. Wash basil leaves, pat dry and remove from stem. Measure out 2 cups basil leaves. Lightly toast pine nuts in a dry skillet over medium heat, stirring constantly for about 2 minutes. Place basil, toasted pine nuts, garlic, and ½ cup olive oil in a blender or food processor. Blend together using pulse speed just until blended, about 6 seconds. Add remaining ½ cup olive oil and pulse about 5 seconds longer. Sauce will be a puree consistency.

2. Pour pesto sauce into a large pasta bowl. Add cheese, salt, and coarse ground black pepper to taste.

3. Boil linguine in an 8-quart pot boiling water with 1 tablespoon salt added. Cook pasta al dente. Using a spaghetti spoon, lift the pasta right out of the water and into the pasta bowl. Add ½ cup pasta water or a little more if needed.

4. Toss the pasta and sauce together. Taste test and add any additional seasoning, if desired. Garnish with extra cheese if desired. Serves 4 to 6.

Spaghetti Aglio e Olio
(SPAGHETTI WITH GARLIC AND OIL)

NOTE: *I can guarantee every Italian child grew up with this dish. We had it at least once a week and I can still smell the garlic. Get fresh basil at your grocery, if you do not grow it.*

1 pound angel hair or thin spaghetti
1 tablespoon salt
1 cup reserved pasta water

¾ cup extra virgin or mild olive oil
3 cloves garlic, minced, about 1 tablespoon
⅓ cup fresh basil leaves, chopped
coarse sea salt to taste
freshly ground coarse black pepper to taste

½ cup freshly grated Romano or Parmesan cheese

1. Pour olive oil in large pasta bowl or platter. Add minced garlic and chopped basil. Stir together. Boil pasta in an 8-quart pot boiling water with 1 tablespoon salt added. Angel hair
cooks very fast, about 3 to 4 minutes. Using a spaghetti spoon, lift the pasta right out of the
water and into the pasta platter containing the oil mixture. Add the reserved pasta water and
toss together. Add salt and freshly ground coarse black pepper. Garnish top with ½ cup freshly
grated cheese (more if desired). Serve immediately with hot, crusty Italian bread. Serves 4.

ELIJAH HARPOLE SCHULTZ
HOLDING BASIL

Rosalie Serving Italian

Ziti with Spicy Pesto

NOTE: *This spicy pesto sauce can also be used over thick spaghetti. It is best made with fresh herbs and tomatoes. Toss the cheese into the pasta for a cheesy flavor.*

1 pound ziti
1 tablespoon salt
½ cup reserved pasta water

¼ cup flat-leaf parsley
½ cup fresh basil leaves
2 tablespoons fresh mint leaves
1 tablespoon capers, rinsed and drained
2 cloves fresh garlic, chopped
¼ cup walnuts
⅓ cup extra virgin olive oil

4 fresh plump Roma tomatoes or
   4 regular medium tomatoes, chopped
¼ teaspoon crushed red pepper flakes
½ teaspoon coarse sea salt, or more for taste
¼ teaspoon coarse ground black pepper

2 tablespoons extra virgin olive oil
½ cup grated Pecorino Romano cheese
freshly ground coarse black pepper

1. Boil ziti in an 8-quart pot boiling water with 1 tablespoon salt added. While ziti is cooking make the pesto sauce.

2. Wash parsley, basil, and mint in cool water, pat dry. Place in blender with capers, garlic, walnuts, and olive oil. Pulse together for about 6 seconds, just enough to chop and blend the mixture. Pour pesto in a large pasta bowl. Add the tomatoes, crushed red pepper flakes, and salt and pepper. Toss together.

3. When ziti is cooked *al dente*, drain, reserving ½ cup pasta water. Add ziti and water to bowl with pesto sauce, mix together. Add the olive oil and cheese; toss together. Garnish with freshly ground coarse black pepper. Pass additional cheese at the table if desired. Serves 6.

Linguine with Clam Sauce

NOTE: *An old favorite, Linguine with Clam Sauce is still popular in Italian restaurants. Cheese is usually not served on this particular dish, but the toasted breadcrumbs will work very nicely. Enjoy!*

1 pound linguine pasta
1 tablespoon salt

¾ cup extra virgin olive oil
3 cloves garlic, chopped
1 (10-ounce) can whole baby clams, juice included
1 (6½-ounce) can chopped clams, juice included
⅛ teaspoon dried thyme leaves
¼ teaspoon crushed red pepper flakes, optional

⅔ cup fresh Italian flat-leaf parsley, chopped
freshly ground coarse black pepper to taste
Modiga (Italian Toasted Bread Crumbs) recipe found on page 95

1. Boil linguine in an 8-quart pot boiling water with 1 tablespoon salt, added. While pasta is cooking, sauté garlic in olive oil about 1 to 2 minutes, until golden. Add the clams, clam juice, thyme, and crushed red pepper flakes. Simmer together about 5 minutes.

2. Cook the linguine to *al dente*, 8 to 9 minutes, tasting pasta for tenderness, but still firm. Using a spaghetti spoon, lift the pasta right out of the water and into the saucepan with clam mixture.

3. Add the parsley and heat together for 1 minute. Transfer to large pasta platter and garnish with freshly ground coarse black pepper and the Italian toasted bread crumbs. Serve immediately for best results. Serves 6 to 8.

(Time: 30 Minutes)

Angel Hair Pasta
(WITH LEMON SHRIMP AND ASPARAGUS)

NOTE: *You will love this creamy light dish. The shrimp and asparagus together with the lemon and half-and-half really compliment each other. Serve with your favorite salad and bread and top this off with* **Rosalie's Italian Cream Cake** *recipe found on page 221.*

½ pound angel hair pasta
1 tablespoon salt

1 pound small tender asparagus,
  ends trimmed
2 tablespoons unsalted butter
2 tablespoons extra virgin olive oil
2 cloves garlic, chopped
1 teaspoon coarse sea salt
¼ teaspoon ground black pepper

¾ pound fresh, or frozen deveined shrimp,
  medium-sized
¼ teaspoon crushed red pepper flakes
1½ cups half-and-half
2 tablespoons fresh lemon juice
1 teaspoon lemon zest

1 cup grated Parmesan cheese
freshly ground coarse black pepper,
  for garnish

1. Wash and trim hard ends from asparagus, about I" or more from the bottom, depending on hardness. Cut into thirds and set aside.

2. Place butter and olive oil in large saucepan with asparagus, garlic, and salt and pepper. Sauté the garlic and asparagus together until the asparagus is crisp-tender, about 5 minutes.

3. Add the washed and cleaned shrimp, crushed red pepper flakes, half-and-half, lemon juice, and lemon zest. Simmer 1 to 2 minutes until shrimp is pink. Turn off the heat.

4. Boil the angel hair in a 4-quart pot boiling water with 1 tablespoon salt added, until al dente, 3 to 4 minutes. Do not overcook. Using a spaghetti spoon, lift the pasta right out of the water and place in the saucepan containing the sauce. Add the cheese and toss together.

5. Garnish with freshly ground coarse black pepper and more cheese if desired. Transfer to individual pasta bowls. Serves 4 to 6.

Shrimp Fettuccine

Rosalie's Shrimp Fettuccine

NOTE: *Rope provel cheese is the key to this dish. It can usually be found in the cheese deli. If not, ask your grocer to order it. If still unable to find, use fresh chunk provolone and coarse grate cheese into sauce. Set the table with your best china for this dish and treat your family to a gourmet dinner.*

1 pound fettuccine

1 tablespoon salt

¼ stick butter

¼ cup olive oil

3 cloves garlic, finely chopped

3 cups broccoli florets

2 cups white capped mushrooms, thick-sliced

1½ teaspoons salt

½ teaspoon ground black pepper

2 cups fresh or frozen deveined shrimp, medium-sized

1½ cups crab meat, fresh or imitation

4 cups heavy whipping cream

3 cups grated Parmesan cheese

2 cups rope provel cheese
  or chunk Provolone grated cheese

freshly ground coarse black pepper to taste

Modiga (Italian Toasted Bread Crumbs)
  recipe found on page 95

1. Boil fettuccine in an 8-quart pot boiling water with 1 tablespoon salt added. While fettuccine is cooking, melt butter and olive oil in a 4-quart saucepan. Add garlic, broccoli, mushrooms, and salt and pepper. Stir-fry over medium heat 4 to 5 minutes for crisp-tender vegetables.

2. Add shrimp and crabmeat. Continue to cook together until shrimp is pink, 3 to 4 minutes. Add cream and stir together gently. Add the cheese, 1 cup at a time, stirring slowly until the cheese is melted into the cream. Add rope provel and continue stirring, until cheese is melted. Remove from heat. This sauce can burn easily.

3. When fettuccini is al dente, drain quickly and add to the saucepan with sauce. If saucepan is too small, for both sauce and pasta, divide into two saucepans. Stir together and let simmer about 1 minute.

4. Transfer to large pasta platter, garnish with freshly ground coarse black pepper. Top with Italian toasted bread crumbs. Serves 6.

Basic Risotto

NOTE: *The key to good risotto is the rice. Try a well-known brand such as Arborio or one you like that ends up creamy and al dente. This basic recipe can accompany most stews and some sauces. Like polenta, there are many uses and various additives that enhance this simple dish.*

2 tablespoons olive oil
1 tablespoon butter
½ cup onion, chopped

1 cup uncooked risotto
3½ cups homemade or low-sodium canned beef or chicken broth, divided
½ teaspoon salt, or more for taste
¼ teaspoon ground black pepper

1 tablespoon butter
¼ cup freshly grated Parmesan cheese

1. Sauté onion in olive oil and butter for about 3 minutes, until translucent. Add rice, stirring for 2 to 3 minutes, until the rice absorbs the oil/butter mixture and becomes slightly "toasted." Stir in 1 cup of broth and continue cooking and stirring until liquid is absorbed. Slowly stir in remaining broth 1 cup at a time, cooking and stirring almost constantly, until all liquid is absorbed before adding the next cup. The entire cooking time will take about 20 minutes. Rice should be creamy and slightly firm.

2. Remove from heat and stir in remaining 1 tablespoon butter and cheese. Use the beef broth with this risotto to accompany the ***Roast Pork with Fennel and Garlic*** recipe found on page 181 or the chicken broth with the ***Italian Stuffed Peppers*** recipe found on page 172. Makes about 3 cups rice. Serves 4.

Polenta

NOTE: *This is a basic polenta recipe and wonderful with or without the cheese. The key is to use a good "stone-ground" cornmeal, coarse grind. I use Bob's Red Mill, found in some grocers or specialty stores. Polenta can be put in the refrigerator and fried the next day.*

6 cups water

2 teaspoons salt

1¾ cups yellow cornmeal

3 tablespoons unsalted butter

½ cup grated Parmesan cheese (optional)

1. In large heavy saucepan, bring water to boil. Add salt. Gradually whisk in the cornmeal. Reduce the heat to low and cook, stirring often, until the mixture thickens and the cornmeal is tender, about 15 minutes. Remove from heat and stir in the butter and the cheese, if using. Serve immediately in warm soup bowls and eat as is or top with your favorite sauce. Serves 6 to 8.

Basic Fried Polenta and Sauce

*B*asic Fried Polenta

NOTE: *These fried polenta squares are very tasty hot and sprinkled with cheese or served with the Sauce for Polenta recipe. Use as an appetizer or as a main course if desired. Polenta is so popular in Italy, I have been told you can usually see large "polenta pots" soaking with water on the back porches in Sicily.*

Polenta recipe found on page 153
olive oil for frying
grated Parmesan cheese for garnish
Sauce for Polenta recipe found on page 156

1. Make the basic polenta recipe. Transfer the hot polenta to a 13" x 9" baking dish coated with olive oil. Cover and refrigerator for 2 to 3 hours or overnight. Cut in squares, about 3" x 2" and lift out gently. Fry in hot olive oil, 4 to 5 minutes on each side. Garnish top with grated Parmesan cheese and serve with polenta sauce or your favorite marinara sauce. Serves 8.

Sauce for Polenta

NOTE: *This is a great sauce for fried polenta and actually serves well for basic warm polenta if desired.*

¼ cup olive oil

¼ cup onion, chopped

1 large clove garlic, minced

1 large green pepper, julienne sliced

2 Italian sausage links, sliced into ½" rounds

1 (15-ounce) can diced tomatoes, juice included

1 (8-ounce) can tomato sauce

¼ teaspoon dried basil leaves

½ teaspoon sugar

⅛ teaspoon crushed red pepper flakes

½ teaspoon coarse sea salt

¼ teaspoon ground black pepper

1. Pour olive oil in saucepan. Over medium heat, sauté the onion, garlic, and green pepper until translucent, about 6 minutes. Add the sausage rounds to vegetables, and continue to fry until sausage is no longer pink.

2. Add the diced tomatoes, tomato sauce, basil, sugar, crushed red pepper flakes, and salt and pepper. Simmer together about 10 minutes. Serve over a fried square of polenta. See **Basic Fried Polenta** recipe found on page 155. Serves 6.

Homemade Ravioli
(FRESH PASTA DOUGH)

NOTE: *Everyone should make these at least once. Take one Saturday and make a memory with your son or daughter, making these wonderful fresh ravioli. Set the table with your best tableware and entertain your own family or someone special. Don't be overwhelmed. It may take a little practice, but anyone can do this.*

4 large fresh eggs

1 teaspoon olive oil

¼ cup water

3 cups all-purpose flour, plus additional for dusting

1 teaspoon salt

1 beaten egg

1 tablespoon water

Ricotta/Spinach Filling recipe found on page 160 or **Meat Filling (for Ravioli)** recipe found on page 159

Marinara Sauce recipe found on page 127

cornmeal

1 tablespoon salt

freshly grated Parmesan cheese

1. Crack the eggs into a bowl, add the olive oil and water and beat until fluffy. In large bowl mix the flour and salt and make a "well" in the middle of the flour. Add the egg mixture a little at a time, mixing in some of the flour. Set this mixture to side of bowl and continue in this manner until all eggs and flour have been used. Continue to bring all the dough together until a ball is formed. Add a little flour if the dough is too sticky to handle. Knead the dough for 8 to 10 minutes, until the dough is smooth and elastic. Put the dough into a plastic bag and refrigerate at least 30 minutes to allow the gluten to relax.

2. After the dough has rested, cut the dough into 6 equal pieces, about 4 ounces each. Keep the dough covered with plastic wrap while working with 1 section of dough at a time. Flatten the section of dough with your hands and flour lightly on both sides. On a lightly floured surface, roll the dough out with a wooden rolling pin, turning often and dusting with flour as needed. Roll the dough very thin into a large rectangle or circle, about 12" to 14". You should see the imprint of your hand through the dough. Beat egg with water until it is foamy. Brush one-half of the dough lightly with the egg wash. Place the filling by teaspoon size on the brushed half of the dough starting at the top, about I" apart and continue to bottom and to the edge of the dough sheet. Make three rows, about 15 doles of filling. Take the unbrushed half of the dough, stretching if necessary, and bring it over to cover the filling. Seal the edge. With your finger, press the dough together down the middle of the rows, removing as much air as you can.

(**Homemade Ravioli** . . . continued on page 158)

(**Homemade Ravioli**... continued from page 157)

3. With a ravioli or pastry cutter, cut the dough down the middle of the rows and then again between each pocket. This should make fifteen 2" ravioli. Place on cookie sheet sprinkled with cornmeal and place in freezer if not using immediately. Let freeze until firm, about 10 minutes, then place in a gallon freezer bag until ready for use. Each section of dough should make 12 to 15 ravioli, totaling about 90 ravioli for the entire recipe batch.

4. Boil the ravioli in an 8-quart pot boiling water with 1 tablespoon salt added. Drop gently about 10 at a time for 5 minutes. Place the lid on the boiling pot midway to steam the ravioli. Remove gently with slotted spoon, place on large platter.

5. Continue to boil ravioli until you have the desired amount for the servings needed. Dress with marinara sauce. Garnish liberally with freshly grated Parmesan cheese. Entire recipe serves 10 to 12. This dough works great for any shape pasta. Use the hand method or a pasta machine if you have one.

Meat Filling
(FOR HOMEMADE RAVIOLI)

NOTE: *Homemade ravioli can be made with many different fillings. This recipe is very traditional, but any variation of ground meat such as ground veal, chicken, beef, or even the combination of all three can be used. Serve with* **Marinara Sauce** *recipe found on page 127. Enjoy!*

½ pound ground chuck
¼ pound ground pork
2 to 3 tablespoons olive oil for frying
1 teaspoon salt
¼ teaspoon ground black pepper
1 cup low-sodium canned chicken broth

1 egg, beaten
1 large clove garlic, minced
¼ cup fresh Italian flat-leaf parsley, chopped
¼ cup grated Parmesan or Pecorino Romano cheese
bread crumbs, if needed
salt and pepper to taste
Homemade Ravioli recipe found on pages 157 and 158

1. In a bowl, mix the ground chuck and ground pork until thoroughly infused together. Brown meat in olive oil, adding salt and pepper, until meat is no longer pink. Add the chicken broth and simmer about 10 minutes, until liquid is absorbed. Remove from heat and let cool.

2. Add the egg, garlic, parsley, and cheese. Add a few bread crumbs if mixture is too moist. Mix together, adding any additional salt and pepper if desired. Put the mixture in a food processor and pulse 1 to 2 minutes, until the meat is pureed. If you do not have a food processor or blender, squeeze the meat with your hands several times until the filling comes together in a smooth consistency. Use immediately or freeze for later use. Use in **Homemade Ravioli** recipe.

Ricotta and Spinach Filling

(FOR HOMEMADE RAVIOLI)

NOTE: *This is a great filling, not only for ravioli, but for other recipes, such as layered between eggplant, lasagna, veal, or chicken.*

1½ cups ricotta cheese
2 cups fresh spinach

¾ cup grated Parmesan cheese
½ cup shredded mozzarella cheese
¼ cup fresh Italian flat-leaf parsley, chopped
1 egg
½ teaspoon salt, or more for your taste
ground black pepper to taste
⅛ teaspoon freshly grated nutmeg

1. Put ricotta in bowl. Blanch the spinach in boiling water 30 seconds. Drain, chop, and add to ricotta.

2. Add the remaining ingredients and mix thoroughly until the mixture is smooth. Use immediately or store in refrigerator up to 1 week. Makes enough for 1 **Homemade Ravioli** recipe found on pages 157 and 158.

Gnocchi with Ricotta
(RICOTTA DUMPLINGS)

NOTE: *Gnocchi can also be made with potatoes, but I love them made with the ricotta cheese. They should be very light and airy. Serve immediately for best results or freeze right after making or they will become mushy. This is a wonderful Italian classic that everyone should experience at least once.*

1 (16-ounce) carton ricotta cheese (2 cups)
3 eggs
½ cup grated Parmesan cheese
2 cups flour, or more if needed
1 tablespoon melted butter

1 tablespoon salt

1. Spoon the ricotta out into a large mixing bowl. Add eggs, cheese, flour and butter. Knead the mixture until dough comes together. If too soft, add a little more flour. Cover bowl with towel and let rest for about 1 hour.

2. Sprinkle flour on work surface and with floured hands, take small amounts of dough and roll gently with both hands to form a long rope, about ½" thick. Set rope of dough aside and continue making the ropes until dough is used up. Cut the ropes crosswise into ½" pieces. Sprinkle the pieces with flour then roll each piece between your palms into a small ball. Place the dough ball on floured surface and with edge of fork press ball with fork tins to make 3 little indentations, rolling the dough as you go to form a little tubular dumpling. Set the gnocchi on floured waxed paper or on a floured towel over a cookie sheet. Continue making all the gnocchi until completed, sifting a little flour over the gnocchi to keep them from sticking. These gnocchi can be used immediately or frozen on the cookie sheets. Place in freezer bags to keep apart.

3. Boil gnocchi in an 8-quart pot boiling water with 1 tablespoon salt added. Drop the gnocchi into the boiling water a few at a time, stirring gently and continuously with a slotted spoon. After they rise to the surface and roll over, cook 2 to 3 minutes longer. The gnocchi can be gently drained, or with slotted spoon, taken directly from boiling water. Place into a large saucepan filled with your favorite sauce.

4. Use **Rosalie's Red Sauce with Meat #1** recipe found on pages 122 and 123, or **Rosalie's Fettuccine Alfredo Sauce** recipe found on page 133. Both are absolutely wonderful with these special little dumplings. Serves 8.

Meat, Fish and Chicken

Meat: Much has been said about the Mediterranean diet, which includes little meat, more fish and chicken, and of course low-saturated fats such as pure olive oil. This type of eating is not only good for us, but the entrees are usually delicious and light. However, like many Italians, my father loved his beef, pork, and veal dishes. He did not feel that a meal was complete without a portion of meat. I can remember him cooking **Grilled Modiga Strip Steaks** and **Spiedini**, piled up on long skewers and served with **Italian Peppermint Sauce.** The flavored smoke would bring the neighbors out and my father would invite half the neighborhood for barbeque. The truth is, they really came and my mother would be scrambling around for more meat to put on the grill. In the winter, when he couldn't grill, my mother would make **Italian Breaded Pork Chops,** loaded with garlic, cheese and parsley. She would make tender **Veal Osso Buco** and **Italian Roast**. Because my father was a butcher, we always had the finest of meats and of course he always made his **Homemade Italian Salsiccia**, which I have included in this section in his memory.

Fish: Although my memory of fish entrees is not as keen as the beef, pork, and chicken, I can remember having fresh **Baked Codfish** topped with a tomato sauce. Two of the best recipes in this section are the **Italian Stuffed Tilapia** and the **Roasted Salmon in Butter and Herbs.** Both are simply delicious. For best results, get the freshest fish you can buy.

Chicken: In Italy, chickens are plentiful and as stated before, it is believed Italians eat more poultry and fish than red meat. Since my mother had a passion for raising and butchering her own chickens, as long as I can remember, we had fresh chicken. She loved fresh chicken soup, and although I didn't realize it at the time, she probably made what we call today **Italian Wedding Soup**. I can remember her making the tiny meatballs and adding them to her chicken broth. The results were wonderful. Another great dish is **Italian Sautéed Chicken Breasts.** Used alone, in salads or in Alfredo sauces, they are excellent. You will also want to try the **Chicken Piccata** and the **Italian Breaded Chicken Rolls.**

Tips: The key to getting the best results when cooking any meat, fish, or chicken entrées, is to be sure to get the best cuts of meat, such as lean ground beef, tender cuts of steaks, fresh chicken, and fish from the market, if possible. Another key is flavoring the meat before cooking. You will notice that in most recipes, I use a coarse ground garlic salt with parsley added. The best I have found is Lawry's.

Grilled Steak over Arugula

Grilled Steak Over Arugula

NOTE: *Arugula can now be found at many grocery stores, but you may need assistance. It looks like a spinach leaf, but has a peppery flavor, which makes this dish wonderful. If you do not have a grill, sear the steaks in hot oil in a fry pan about 2 minutes on each side. Turn only once and proceed as indicated below.*

2 - 1 pound rib-eye steaks, about 1" thick
2 to 3 tablespoons olive oil
coarse garlic salt with dried parsley
coarse ground black pepper

4 cups baby arugula leaves, washed and drained dry
¼ cup extra virgin olive oil
1 tablespoon balsamic vinegar
1 teaspoon coarse sea salt
freshly ground coarse black pepper

1. Rub steaks with olive oil and sprinkle liberally with the coarse garlic salt. Sprinkle lightly with the coarse ground pepper. Grill the steaks over an open grill for 3 to 4 minutes on each side. This dish seems to have more flavor if the steaks are cooked to no more than medium rare. Transfer steaks to a platter so juices can be saved and let steak rest for about 5 minutes. Cut steaks into 2" x 1" pieces.

2. Arrange the arugula on a large platter. Whisk together the olive oil and balsamic vinegar. Pour over the arugula. Sprinkle with the salt and freshly ground coarse black pepper to taste. Place the steak pieces with juice over the greens. Serve with warm Italian bread to dip in juices. Serves 4.

Italian Sausage
(WITH PEPPERS AND ONIONS)

NOTE: *Excellent made into sandwiches on Italian bread and topped with a slice of mozzarella or Provolone cheese. Place under broiler until cheese melts. Top with other slice of bread.*

3 peppers, red and yellow combined

¼ cup olive oil

1 small onion sliced

2 cloves garlic, chopped

2 Italian sausage links, sliced into ½" thick round slices

½ teaspoon coarse sea salt, or more to taste

¼ teaspoon coarse ground black pepper, or more to taste

1. Wash, core, and seed peppers. Cut in julienne pieces, not too thin. Place peppers in saucepan with olive oil, onion, and garlic. Sauté over medium heat for about 2 minutes.

2. Add the sausage and sauté both over medium heat 8 to 10 minutes, until the peppers are tender and the sausage is browned. Salt and pepper to taste. Serve as is or over bread for sandwiches. Can also be used over ¼ pound of short noodles, such as farfalle. Serves 4.

Rosalie's Italian Meatloaf

NOTE: *This meatloaf is absolutely delicious and can be served with* **Basic Risotto** *recipe found on page 152, or even penne pasta. This is another great Sunday afternoon meal.*

2 pounds lean ground beef
1 pound lean ground pork

1 cup plain bread crumbs
½ cup Pecorino Romano cheese, grated
2 eggs
½ cup whole tomatoes, chopped fine, juice included
1 (8-ounce) can tomato sauce
½ cup finely chopped onion
⅓ cup Italian flat-leaf parsley, chopped
1 teaspoon crushed red pepper flakes
1 tablespoon salt
1 teaspoon coarse ground black pepper
olive oil for oiling pan

Marinara Sauce recipe found on page 127

1. Preheat oven to 375°F. In large bowl, mix the ground beef and ground pork with your hands until blended together. Add the bread crumbs, cheese, eggs, whole tomatoes, tomato sauce, onion, parsley, crushed red pepper flakes, and salt and pepper. Mix together, crushing the whole tomatoes with your hands as you go. Place meat in large oiled baking pan and shape into one large loaf, evenly distributing the meat.

2. Bake uncovered in oven for 1 hour and 10 minutes or until meat thermometer inserted into meat registers 160°.

3. Prepare homemade marinara sauce and when meatloaf has been in the oven 30 minutes, remove. Spread 3/4 cup marinara sauce over meat and return to oven for remainder time of 40 minutes.

4. Remove pan from oven and transfer to table onto hot plate. Let meat rest about 5 to 10 minutes. Slice and serve. Place remaining marinara sauce in large bowl on table. Sauce can be spooned over sliced meatloaf, if desired. Serves 10.

Italian Hamburgers

Italian Hamburgers

NOTE: *This juicy Italian hamburger is something that you will not want to miss. It is simply delicious. Serve as a main entree or as sandwiches with Italian bread. Top with provolone cheese, tomato slice, and purple onion rings.*

1½ pounds ground chuck or sirloin

3 cloves garlic, chopped

⅓ cup plain bread crumbs

⅓ cup Parmesan cheese

¼ cup fresh curly parsley, chopped

3 eggs

½ teaspoon fennel seeds

1 teaspoon salt

¼ teaspoon ground black pepper

olive oil

1. Mix together the ground meat, garlic, bread crumbs, cheese, parsley, eggs, fennel seeds, and salt and pepper. Fry in olive oil over medium heat 4 to 5 minutes on each side. Makes 6 large patties.

(Time: 1 Hour and 30 Minutes,
plus 3 to 4 Hours for resting)

Italian Homemade Salsiccia
(ITALIAN SAUSAGE)

NOTE: *If you do not have a meat grinder or attachments, you can still make this sausage in bulk form by making sausage patties. This recipe is in memory of my father, William Fiorino, who made this wonderful homemade sausage for the enjoyment of our family, friends, and neighbors. If you make this once, you will make it again and again.*

1 meat grinder with funnel attachment

4 pounds ground boneless pork butt, fat untrimmed
2 pounds ground beef
1 cup Pecorino Romano cheese, grated
1 (15-ounce) can whole tomatoes chopped fine, juice included
3 tablespoons fennel seed
2 teaspoons crushed red pepper flakes
2 tablespoons salt
1 teaspoon coarse ground black pepper

25 feet pork casing

1. Grind meat in meat grinder or have your meat cutter do it. In large bowl, mix together the ground pork butt, ground beef, cheese, tomatoes, fennel seed, crushed red pepper flakes, and salt and pepper. Mix together well. Cover with plastic wrap and leave refrigerated for 3 to 4 hours to let rest and combine flavors.

2. Clean casing by pushing about 1" of one end of the casing over the spout of faucet in your sink, making sure the rest of the casing remains in the sink. Turn on water and gently wash out casing to remove any preserving salts or residue. Remove casing from spout. When meat is ready to stuff, use the stuffing attachment on your meat grinder to make sausage links. Twist the sausage into 3½" links as you go. Makes 6 pounds of sausage.

Grilled Modiga Strip Steaks

NOTE: *My father, William Fiorino, grilled these steaks outside during the summer. They are a lot like Spiedinis, only not rolled and stuffed.*

4 strip sirloin steaks
coarse ground garlic salt with parsley
½ cup olive oil

1 cup plain bread crumbs
½ cup grated Parmesan, or Pecorino Romano cheese
3 cloves garlic, minced
¼ cup fresh curly parsley, chopped
1 teaspoon coarse sea salt
¼ teaspoon ground black pepper

Italian Peppermint Sauce recipe found on page 120

1. Rinse steaks in cool water. Pat dry and sprinkle liberally with garlic salt. Pour olive oil in large shallow dish and coat steaks on both sides. Leave steaks in oil and set aside.

2. Mix bread crumbs, cheese, garlic, parsley, and salt and pepper together. Place bread crumbs in a large shallow dish. Dip oil-coated steaks in bread crumb mixture on both sides. Place on hot grill, about 2 to 3 minutes on each side. Return steaks to large platter. Serve with Italian peppermint sauce. In winter months, charbroil steaks under broiler 2 to 3 minutes, turning once. Being careful not to overcook. Serves 4.

WILLIAM FIORINO — ROSALIE'S FATHER

Italian Stuffed Peppers

NOTE: *These peppers are awesome, with plenty of sauce for everyone. The colors over the rice will make the dish very impressive. Serve with risotto and hot bread.*

4 medium green bell peppers

1 pound lean hamburger
¼ cup grated Parmesan cheese
¼ cup plain bread crumbs
2 cloves garlic, chopped
2 tablespoons fresh curly parsley, chopped
2 eggs
1 teaspoon salt
¼ teaspoon pepper
½ cup olive oil, divided

½ cup celery, diced
⅓ cup onion, chopped

1 (15-ounce) can diced tomatoes,
   juice included
1 teaspoon sugar
½ teaspoon dried basil leaves
½ teaspoon salt
¼ teaspoon ground black pepper
1 (15-ounce) can tomato sauce

3 cups cooked rice,
   or **Basic Risotto** recipe, (chicken flavored)
   found on page 152

parsley sprigs for garnish, if desired

1. Preheat oven to 350°F. Core peppers and cut each one in half. Remove inside seeds and ribs. Wash the peppers and set aside.

2. Mix the hamburger, cheese, bread crumbs, garlic, parsley, eggs, and salt and pepper in a large bowl. Divide the meat among the peppers, filling each half. In a large saucepan over medium heat, brown the filled peppers in ¼ cup olive oil, turning once to brown, about 3 minutes on each side. If all the peppers do not fit on the first browning, divide them until all are browned. Place peppers in large deep baking dish. Set aside.

3. In remaining olive oil, brown the celery and onion until translucent, 4 to 5 minutes. Add the tomatoes, sugar, basil, and salt and pepper. Simmer 5 minutes then add the tomato sauce. Simmer another 5 minutes. Remove from heat and pour sauce over peppers in baking dish.

4. Cover with foil and bake 30 minutes. Boil rice to make 3 cups. Remove the peppers when hot and bubbly and arrange over the rice on a large platter. Garnish with parsley sprigs. Serves 4 to 6.

Brozzaloni
(STUFFED ROLLED STEAK)

NOTE: *This is an Italian classic, usually meant for a Sunday afternoon meal or for a special occasion. This is a beautiful meal worth your time. It is my sister-in-law's, Rose Marie Fiorino's recipe.*

1 large round steak, pounded
　as thin as possible
2 tablespoons olive oil
coarse garlic salt with parsley

½ cup plain bread crumbs
½ cup Parmesan cheese
2 cloves garlic, minced
2 tablespoons fresh curly parsley, chopped
½ teaspoon salt
¼ teaspoon ground black pepper

1¼ cups sweet Italian sausage, browned
1 cup rope provel cheese,
　or 3 slices provolone cheese

3 hard boiled eggs, peeled
kitchen string
olive oil
Red Sauce with Meat #2 recipe found
　on pages 122 and 123 , for a large crowd

1. Lay round steak on work surface and pound with meat mallet, until preferably ⅛" thick, and evenly flat. Brush with olive oil on both sides and sprinkle liberally with the coarse garlic salt.

2. Mix the bread crumbs, cheese, garlic, parsley, and salt and pepper, until well blended. Spread evenly over the oiled round steak.

3. Take sausage out of casing and brown lightly in saucepan; do not cook completely. Lay crumbled sausage over breadcrumbs. Next, add the rope provel or provolone slices. Make a small indenture across the middle of the layered steak horizontally and place the hard boiled eggs end to end. The idea is, when the steak is sliced, a slice of egg will appear, neatly rounded. After the eggs are placed, starting at the end of steak, roll jelly-roll style over the eggs first, then continue to roll until folded over. Tie each end and in the middle with kitchen string, so that the stuffed steak is secure. In large saucepan, sear the rolled steak in olive oil on all sides. The steak can now be placed right in the pot of the red meat sauce and left to simmer for at least 1½ hours. Omit the sausage and half of the pork ribs normally called for in the red sauce recipe to make room for the large stuffed steak.

4. When the sauce is completed cooking, and steak is tender, remove and place on large meat platter. Slice the stuffed steak in 1" slices. You should have a pretty slice of egg in the center. Surround the stuffed steak with the meatballs from the sauce. Serve with penne pasta for an impressive, beautiful meal. Serves 8 to 10.

Italian Roast
(WITH ONIONS AND PEPPERS)

NOTE: *This roast can also simmer in its sauce slowly on top of the stove in a large saucepan for 3 hours. The sauce is rich and sweet because of the vegetables. If you do not like green peppers, add another onion and 1 cup chopped celery.*

3½ pounds chuck roast, or eye round roast
1 large clove garlic
coarse garlic salt with dried parsley
flour
olive oil

¼ cup olive oil
2 medium onions, chopped
1 large green pepper, cored,
  seeded and chopped
½ cup chopped celery

1 (28-ounce) can whole tomatoes
1 (6-ounce) can tomato paste

1 can rinse water from tomato paste
1 cup homemade or low-sodium
  canned beef broth

1 teaspoon sugar
½ teaspoon dried basil
1 tablespoon fresh Italian
  flat-leaf parsley, chopped
1 teaspoon salt
¼ teaspoon ground black pepper

½ pound farfalle (bow tie) pasta, (optional)

1. Preheat oven 350°F. Rinse roast, pat dry, and trim any fat. Cut garlic clove in 3 slivers and embed in roast with sharp knife in 3 different places. Sprinkle liberally with garlic salt and coat with flour. In large saucepan, sear roast in hot oil on both sides, 8 to 10 minutes. Remove from pan.

2. In same large sauce pan, add the ¼ cup olive oil and sauté the onion, green pepper, and celery, about 15 minutes, until the vegetables are golden. Remove any hard stems from tomatoes and chop fine. Pour tomatoes with juice over vegetables. Stir in the tomato paste, water and beef broth. Add the sugar, basil, parsley, and salt and pepper. Simmer about 10 minutes. Pour over roast and bake covered with lid or foil for about 2 hours. Remove from oven when roast is very tender. Skim off any collected oil from top of sauce.

3. Slice the roast in thin slices and return to sauce. Taste, and add more seasonings if desired. Serve over farfalle pasta, if desired. Boil according to package directions. Serves 6 to 8.

Spiedini

Spiedini
(STUFFED MEAT ROLLS)

NOTE: *I can't describe how delicious these little stuffed meat rolls are. You just have to experience it for yourself. Get a good soft provolone cheese fresh from the deli, and also get freshly cut Genoa salami. The peppermint sauce sends these spiedinis over the top. You will make these again and again.*

1-3 pound top round roast, sliced in very thin
  steaks, about ⅛" thick or less, or 12 very thin
  breakfast steaks
coarse garlic salt with dried parsley
1 cup olive

12 slices Genoa salami,
  sliced fresh from the deli
12 slices Provolone cheese,
  sliced fresh from the deli
olive oil

1 cup plain bread crumbs
1 cup Pecorino Romano grated cheese
3 cloves garlic, minced
¼ cup fresh curly parsley, chopped
1 teaspoon coarse sea salt
½ teaspoon ground black pepper

1. Heat grill or preheat oven to 350°F. Have your meat cutter slice steaks thin from roast, or pound steaks between waxed paper until very thin, about 1/8" thick or less. Steaks should be about 5" long and 3" to 4" wide. Sprinkle steaks liberally with garlic salt. Pour the olive oil in a baking dish and coat the steaks well on both sides, leaving the steaks in the olive oil while preparing the bread crumbs. Mix together the bread crumbs, cheese, garlic, parsley, and salt and pepper.

2. Work with one steak at a time. Put each steak in the bread crumb mixture, and coat both sides heavily, pressing the bread crumbs into the meat. Place one piece of salami, and one slice of the provolone cheese, on each steak. Starting at one end of the steak, roll the meat up tight, jelly-roll style, while tucking in the cheese. Secure rolls with tooth-picks. Pierce each roll with two long skewers, about 4 rolls to the skewers. Place on hot grill 3 to 5 minutes on each side, or bake the rolls on a large cookie sheet with rack, for 20 to 25 minutes, being careful not to overcook. Drizzle a little additional olive over the top while they are baking. Bake until brown and bubbly. Transfer to platter, and serve with *Italian Peppermint Sauce* recipe found on page 120. It is likely you will get 12 thin steaks from each roast. Serves 6.

Osso Buco
(BRAISED VEAL SHANKS)

NOTE: *Osso buco means "bone with hole" pertaining to the bone marrow on the shank. Italians eat this bone marrow as a delicacy. It is a very rich and savory dish. Ask your meat cutter to order veal shanks, and be prepared for an expensive treasure, saving this dish for special guests.*

4 veal shanks, 2" thick slices, about 1 pound each

coarse garlic salt with dried parsley

ground black pepper

½ cup flour

3 to 4 tablespoons olive oil, or more if needed

½ cup water

¼ cup olive oil

1 medium onion chopped

3 cloves garlic, minced

2 stalks celery with leaves, chopped ½" slices

1 large carrot, ¼" slices

1 teaspoon coarse sea salt

½ teaspoon coarse ground black pepper

2 tablespoons tomato paste

4 cups homemade or low-sodium canned chicken broth

1 sprig fresh thyme or ½ teaspoon dried

1 bay leaf

¼ cup fresh Italian flat-leaf parsley, chopped

1. Preheat oven to 375°F. Wash and pat dry veal shanks. Sprinkle all sides with garlic salt and pepper and roll the shanks in the flour to coat. In large fry pan, heat the oil and brown the shanks on all sides, 6 to 8 minutes per side. The meat should have a crusty brown coating. Transfer the shanks to a large roasting pan. Deglaze the searing pan with ½ cup water. Heat the water to gather the meat bits and juice and pour over meat.

2. In a clean fry pan, pour the ¼ cup olive oil and sauté the onion, garlic, celery, and carrot. Sprinkle with salt and pepper while frying for about 8 minutes. Add the tomato paste and work into the vegetables. Add the vegetables to the roaster with the chicken broth, fresh thyme, bay leaf, and parsley.

3. Cover the pan with lid or aluminum foil and braise in the oven for about 1½ hours. Turn the veal shanks over once or twice during cooking. The meat should be fork-tender. Transfer to a large platter and place the vegetables all around the meat. Traditionally served with **Gremolada Sauce** recipe as found on page 179. Serves 4.

Gremolada Sauce
(FOR OSSO BUCO)

NOTE: *Gremolada is a strong-flavored garnish that can add flavor to a dish; however, too much can take it away. This is a classic sauce that usually accompanies **Osso Buco** recipe found on page 178, but is not necessarily essential.*

1 tablespoon lemon zest, minced
2 tablespoons fresh Italian flat-leaf parsley, minced
1 small clove garlic, minced.

1. Mix the lemon zest, parsley, and garlic together. Use sparingly over *Osso Buco*.

Veal Parmigiana

NOTE: *This dish is the classic Italian-American veal dish, served at many Italian restaurants. The veal cutlets are tender and flavorful and can be found in most grocery meat sections.*

6 veal cutlets, thin sliced
2 eggs, beaten
Italian Bread Crumbs recipe found on page 94
olive oil

Marinara Sauce recipe found on page 127
½ cup grated Parmesan cheese, more if desired
6 slices mozzarella cheese
parsley sprigs for garnish

1. Preheat oven to 400°F. Prepare bread crumbs and place in shallow plate. Dip cutlets in eggs and then in bread crumbs on both sides to coat evenly. Fry in hot oil about 2 minutes on each side.

2. Using a 13" X 9" baking dish, pour ½ to ¾ cup marinara sauce in bottom. Without overlapping, place chops on sauce in one even layer. Cover with 1 to 2 cups marinara sauce and sprinkle sauce with grated Parmesan cheese. Place 1 slice of mozzarella cheese over each cutlet.

3. Bake uncovered 8 to 10 minutes until cheese melts and sauce is bubbly. Serve in baking dish garnished with parsley sprigs. Serves 6.

Roast Pork Loin
(WITH FENNEL AND GARLIC)

NOTE: *The garlic and fennel embedded into the roast, gives the meat a distinct flavor, not too heavy, but notable. Serve with beef-flavored risotto for a hearty meal.*

1-3 pound pork roast

2 medium cloves garlic, peeled and sliced into thirds

1 teaspoon fennel seed

coarse garlic salt with dried parsley

¼ teaspoon ground black pepper

1 teaspoon ground fennel

flour

¼ cup olive oil for searing

1 large onion, small quartered

2 stalks celery, cut into ½" slices

6 to 8 baby carrots

1 (8-ounce) package white button mushrooms, rinsed and left whole, stems removed

1 teaspoon salt

¼ teaspoon ground black pepper

2 cups homemade or low-sodium canned beef broth

2 tablespoons flour

½ cup water

1. Preheat oven to 350°F. Rinse roast under cool water; pat dry. Insert six holes with sharp tip of knife in various places in the roast. Put a sliver of garlic in each hole. Make four additional holes and place ¼ teaspoon fennel seeds in each hole. Sprinkle all sides of roast with the coarse garlic salt and pepper. Rub all over with ground fennel. Coat the roast evenly with the flour and sear in hot oil in large saucepan on all sides. Remove roast to a 9" x 13" baking pan.

2. Place the onion, celery, carrots, and mushrooms around the roast. Sprinkle the salt and pepper on the vegetables. Add the beef broth and roast uncovered in the oven for about 1½ hours. Pork should bake for 25 to 30 minutes per pound. Remove when tender or when thermometer placed in thick part of roast reads 175°.

3. Transfer roast to large platter. Put remaining vegetables and juice in large saucepan and bring to boil. Add the flour to cool water; mix to make a smooth consistency. Add the flour mixture to the juice to make a smooth gravy and simmer until thickened. Add any additional salt or pepper if desired. Place the vegetables and gravy around the roast. Serve with **Basic Risotto (beef-flavored)** recipe found on page 152. Serves 6.

Italian Breaded Pork and Brussels Sprouts

Italian Breaded Pork or Veal Chops

NOTE: *Whether pork or veal, these chops are delicious. Served with **Sautéed Brussels Sprouts** found on page 84, or your favorite side dish, it could be one of my favorite Italian meals. They also work well in the **Veal Parmigiana** recipe found on page 180.*

4 pork or veal chops ¼" to ½" thick

coarse garlic salt with dried parsley

2 eggs, well beaten

Italian Bread Crumbs recipe found on page 94

olive oil

1. Rinse meat off in cool water; pat dry. Sprinkle chops on both sides with coarse garlic salt. Dip chops into eggs and then bread crumb mixture until well coated. Fry in olive oil in large saucepan over medium heat 5 to 6 minutes on each side. Cover pan with lid and steam low for about 8 minutes. Using spatula, remove chops to platter, careful to keep breading intact. The chops should be very tender and juicy. Serves 4.

Italian Crusted Chicken

NOTE: *This is my Italian version of fried chicken. It is crusted on the outside and juicy on the inside. A very delicious entree that is great served with **Italian Roasted Vegetables** recipe found on page 76.*

4 skinless chicken breasts, boneless
coarse garlic salt with parsley

1 cup flour
2 tablespoons grated Parmesan cheese
¼ teaspoon paprika
1 teaspoon salt
½ teaspoon pepper

oil olive for frying
parsley sprigs for garnish

1. Rinse chicken breast in cold water and pat dry. Remove any fat or hard gristle. Cut each chicken breast in half for smaller portions. Sprinkle chicken liberally with garlic salt.

2. Combine the flour, cheese, paprika, and salt and pepper in a shallow bowl. Coat chicken on both sides with the flour mixture. In large saucepan, fry chicken in olive oil over medium heat 4 to 5 minutes on each side. Place lid on pan and turn heat to medium-low. Let chicken steam for about 8 minutes. Transfer to platter and garnish with parsley sprigs. This dish is best served while it is still hot and crunchy. Serves 4 to 6.

Garlic Sautéed Chicken

NOTE: *This recipe needs no other seasoning; just enjoy it in its simplicity.*

4 skinless chicken breasts, boneless
coarse ground garlic salt with dried parsley
fine ground black pepper
olive oil for frying

1. Rinse and pat the chicken dry. Remove any hard gristle or fat. Sprinkle liberally with coarse garlic salt and lightly season with pepper. Pour olive oil in large saucepan and sauté chicken breasts over medium heat, about 5 minutes on each side. Cover pan and steam 6 to 8 minutes. Arrange on platter and garnish with parsley sprigs. Serve with vegetable and salad of your choice. Serves 4.

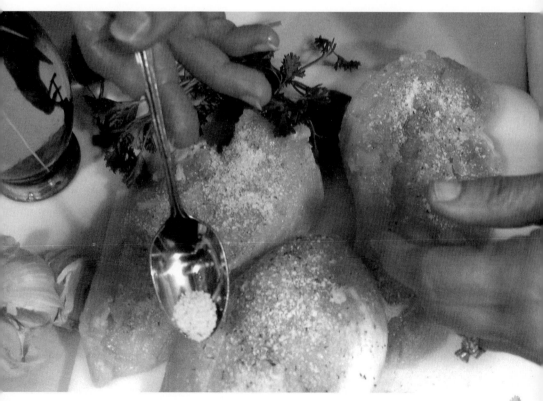

Italian Breaded Chicken Rolls

Italian Breaded Chicken Rolls
(CHICKEN SALTIMBOCCA)

NOTE: *These wonderful little rolls will have your taste buds hopping; they are awesome! Adopted from the Roman dish, Veal Saltimbocca, using chicken fillets instead. Saltimbocca means "leap in the mouth."*

6 thin skinless chicken fillets

olive oil

coarse garlic salt with dried parsley

1 (10-ounce) package frozen
  chopped spinach, thawed and drained

2 tablespoons olive oil

salt and pepper

6 thin slices prosciutto

1 cup rope provel cheese, divided
  or 6 slices buffalo mozzarella

2 beaten eggs

½ cup Progresso Italian Style bread crumbs

½ cup grated Parmesan cheese

2 cloves garlic, minced

2 tablespoons fresh Italian
  flat-leaf parsley, chopped.

⅓ cup olive, more if needed

coarse sea salt to taste

ground black pepper to taste

freshly grated Parmesan cheese for garnish

1. Rinse chicken fillets well, pat dry, and place on work surface. Fillets should be about ⅛" thick. If too thick, pound the fillets between waxed paper to flatten thin and evenly. Brush olive oil on both sides and sprinkle with the coarse garlic salt.

2. Squeeze the thawed spinach to remove any excess water and place in bowl. Add olive oil with a little salt and pepper to flavor the spinach. Toss together. Place 1 slice of prosciutto over each fillet. Next, add about 1 tablespoon flavored spinach over prosciutto. Lastly, add some rope provel or mozzarella. Starting from one end, roll the fillets up jelly-roll style and secure with a strong toothpick.

3. Beat the eggs until fluffy. Mix bread crumbs, cheese, garlic and parsley. Lay bread crumb mixture in a shallow bowl. Dip each roll into eggs, then into the bread crumbs. Fry in hot olive oil in large saucepan, about 4 to 5 minutes on each side until golden brown. Turn heat down and put lid on pan to steam the rolls, 8 to 10 minutes. Remove the breaded rolls to a large platter.

4. Sprinkle with a little coarse sea salt, pepper, and grated Parmesan cheese. Serve as is, or with your favorite marinara or Alfredo sauce spooned over each roll. Serves 6.

Chicken Piccata

NOTE: *This is a popular dish, with just enough lemon to make the palate pop. This butter/lemon sauce can also be used over baked fish.*

4 skinless chicken breasts, boneless
coarse garlic salt with dried parsley
½ cup all-purpose flour

¼ cup extra virgin olive oil
3 tablespoons unsalted butter

½ cup homemade or low-sodium chicken broth
¼ cup fresh squeezed lemon juice, plus 1 teaspoon
¼ cup capers, drained and rinsed
¼ cup Italian flat-leaf parsley, chopped

coarse black pepper to taste
1 tablespoon butter
1 teaspoon lemon juice
parsley sprigs, optional

1. Rinse chicken breasts in cool water; pat dry. Remove any gristle or fat. Sprinkle breasts liberally with garlic salt and coat both sides in flour. Set aside.

2. Heat the oil and butter together in large saucepan over medium heat. Sauté the chicken 4 to 5 minutes on each side until crusted and golden brown. Carefully remove chicken using flat server, and place on platter.

3. In same pan, add the chicken broth, lemon juice, capers, and fresh parsley. Scrape bottom of pan and whisk together over low heat. Place the chicken breasts back into the pan and simmer with lid on for 6 to 8 minutes. Remove lid and sprinkle lightly with coarse black pepper.

4. Transfer chicken back to platter carefully with flat server, so as not to remove coating. Add remaining 1 tablespoon butter to sauce and test for taste, adding additional 1 teaspoon lemon juice if desired. Heat together 30 seconds and pour hot sauce over chicken. Garnish platter with parsley sprigs. Serves 4.

Roasted Salmon
(IN BUTTER AND HERBS)

NOTE: *This dish is simply delicious and very rich with flavor. Use a fresh fillet of good salmon for the best taste.*

¼ cup extra virgin olive oil
½ stick butter
2 teaspoons garlic, minced fine

¼ cup fresh Italian flat-leaf parsley, chopped
pinch crushed red pepper flakes
1 teaspoon coarse sea salt
coarse ground black pepper to taste

1 salmon fillet, 2 to 3 pounds

2 tablespoons fresh lemon juice
parsley sprigs for garnish

1. Preheat oven to 400 °F. In a large saucepan place olive oil and butter over medium heat until butter melts and foam subsides. Add the minced garlic and sauté for 1 minute. Add the parsley, red pepper flakes, and salt and pepper. Stir into the butter.

2. Lay the salmon in the butter sauce fillet-side down and skin-side up in pan and sauté gently for 2 minutes. Remove from heat. Cut a large piece of heavy foil, about 12" x 24" and place the salmon fillet-side up on the foil. Pour all the pan juices over the salmon. Wrap the foil up around the salmon and seal.

3. Place on a large cookie sheet and bake for 20 to 25 minutes. The salmon should be pink and flaky.

4. Transfer to large platter and drizzle fresh lemon juice on the top before serving. Garnish with parsley sprigs. Serves 4 to 6.

Italian Stuffed Tilapia

Italian Stuffed Tilapia

NOTE: *A light fish such as flounder or perch may be used in place of tilapia. This dish is not only mouth-watering, but also very beautiful.*

6 tilapia fillets, about 6 ounces each
olive oil
coarse garlic salt with dried parsley

½ cup Progresso Italian Style bread crumbs
⅓ cup grated Parmesan cheese
2 tablespoons fresh Italian flat-leaf parsley, chopped
1 large clove garlic, minced
⅛ teaspoon crushed red pepper flakes
½ teaspoon coarse sea salt
¼ teaspoon ground black pepper

3 tablespoons olive oil
⅓ cup crab meat, chopped

parsley sprigs
freshly squeezed lemon juice

1. Preheat oven to 375°F. Rinse tilapia fillets and pat dry. Coat on both sides with olive oil and sprinkle with coarse garlic salt. Arrange fillets on lightly oiled baking sheet. Set aside.

2. In medium bowl, combine bread crumbs, cheese, parsley, garlic, crushed red pepper flakes, and salt and pepper. Mix together. Add olive oil and crab meat to bread crumb mixture. This should be a moist, but not a "wet" stuffing. Cover each fillet with a portion of the stuffing, about 2 to 3 tablespoons.

3. Bake 10 to 12 minutes until fish is opaque and flakes easily. Use the broiler the last 15 to 20 seconds to form a browned crust, being careful not to burn. Remove each fillet carefully with a spatula onto a pretty platter garnished with parsley sprigs. Squeeze fresh lemon juice over each tilapia fillet. Serves 6.

Breaded Fillet of Fresh Cod
(WITH ITALIAN PEPPERMINT SAUCE)

NOTE: *This is a great recipe for baked fish. If you do not have cod, use a good meaty white fish, such as grouper or perch. The seasoned bread crumbs are tasty enough even if you don't have the peppermint sauce on hand.*

6 fresh cod fillets, 1" thick
2 to 3 tablespoons olive oil
coarse garlic salt with dried parsley

Seasoned Bread Crumbs for Fish recipe found on page 105
Italian Peppermint Sauce recipe found on page 120

1. Preheat oven to 400°F. Brush both sides of cod fillets with olive oil. Sprinkle with coarse garlic salt. Top each fillet with 1 tablespoon of seasoned bread crumbs.

2. Place in a large deep baking dish and bake in oven for 8 to 10 minutes. Fish should turn opaque and flake easily with a fork. Do not overcook or the fish will be dry.

3. Remove and spoon on Italian peppermint sauce over each fillet. Serve from baking dish or arrange on large platter. Serves 6.

Shrimp Scampi

NOTE: *Shrimp scampi is an Italian favorite. If you don't have fresh shrimp, frozen cooked shrimp will do; just don't simmer it very long. Great for appetizers or over **Italian Salad** found on page 56, for a meal in itself.*

1 pound medium fresh shrimp, peeled and deveined
1 tablespoon olive oil
4 tablespoons unsalted butter
2 cloves garlic, minced
¼ cup fresh Italian flat-leaf parsley, chopped
pinch crushed red pepper flakes, optional

2 teaspoons lemon juice, or more to your taste

1. Rinse shrimp in cool water; drain. Place olive oil and butter in large saucepan. Sauté the garlic for about 1 minute. Add the shrimp, parsley, and crushed red pepper flakes. Cook for 1 to 2 minutes, being careful not to overcook. Shrimp will turn pink when done.

2. Add the lemon juice and toss gently. Serves 4 to 6.

Rosalie's Italian Cream Cake

All About Desserts

Desserts in the Italian culinary are distinctive to the province or region of Italy that they come from. Since my mother was from Sicily, her desserts were laced with citrus fruits, almonds, figs, and ricotta, along with flavors of anise and almond. Today, our Italian-American restaurants serve a variety of Italian pastries from all regions of Italy. One favorite is Tiramisù, which could be one of the most popular of Italian desserts. Another characteristic of some of the Italian desserts is the lack of sweetness. Examples are the **Sesame Cookies** or the **Chocolate Almond Biscotti,** which have their own distinct flavor, and yet are very good. Because I like sweet things, I have tried to include a variety of classics such as **Italian Fig Cookies, Italian Cannolis,** and the more American **Italian Cream Cake.** Because of the vast variety of Italian desserts, entire cookbooks have been written on this subject.

TIPS: The best advice that I can give about making top-quality desserts, or any food for that matter, is to have the equipment to do so. The difference between a "fair" dessert and a "great" dessert will mostly depend on the quality of your tools. Use the best that your money can buy, getting one or two pieces at a time until you have a good supply. Heavy-duty pans with a non-stick coating do a good job. Your cakes, cookies, and custards will be lighter, yet firm, and hold their shape.

Basic Pastry Essentials: Pie Pans: Use oven-proof glass 9" x 5" pie pans. Cake pans: You will need three 9" pans and at least one 13" x 9" x 2" baking pan. Cookie sheets: It is always nice to have three or more of various sizes. Metal racks for cooling cakes are wonderful to have and a must. Other gadgets, such as pastry cutters, lemon zesters, a cake and pie slicer, can be added a little at a time. Put your order in for bigger things on your birthday, like a food processor, an electric mixer, blender, or a brand new set of pots and pans.

Other Tools: Measuring devices are items that every cook must have, and no one can have enough. Be sure to have a 4-cup and a 2-cup glass measuring cup, as well as dry measures. Bowls of all sizes will always be used. Also needed are measuring spoons, spatulas, slotted spoons, whisks, and by all means, a wooden rolling pin. Invest in a small scale, you will use it.

Fresh Ingredients: Use fresh eggs for your baking. It really will make a difference. Always use real butter. Clean out your spice cabinet and toss the nutmeg you borrowed from your neighbor years ago. Spices should be replaced every so often and some every six months. For fresh flavor and aroma, keep spices fresh. Always have lemons on hand to sprinkle on fresh fruits to keep them from discoloration.

Patience and Practice: Italian desserts can be simple, as in **Sugared Pecan Balls** or a little more complex, as in **Tiramisù,** but don't hesitate to try them all. Patience and practice will pay off and your family and friends will be so glad you persevered. By all means, make up a batch of **Italian Cream Puffs with Custard Pudding** recipes found on pages 208 and 209. Your children will get up on any Saturday morning ready to do extra chores for a promise of a cream puff.

ROSALIE'S GRANDCHILDREN —
GRANT AND MAX HARPOLE

Sesame Cookies

NOTE: *These cookies are crunchy, and have a taste of their own. They are not overly sweet and have a tendency to get hard. They are perfect for dunking into milk or coffee and Italians love to dip them, especially the next day.*

3 cups flour (a little more if needed)
¼ teaspoon salt
2½ teaspoons baking powder

½ cup butter
1 cup sugar
3 eggs
1 teaspoon vanilla
flour for kneading dough

2 cups sesame seeds
1 cup milk

1. Preheat oven to 350°F. Mix the flour, salt, and baking powder in a small bowl. Set aside.

2. Cream the butter and sugar with electric mixer. Add the eggs and vanilla and beat until fluffy. Add the flour mixture a little at a time and stir into the egg mixture. Using all the flour and egg mixture, bring the dough together into a ball. Knead the dough on floured surface, adding a little more flour if dough is sticky. Pinch off small portions of dough and roll into a rope 8" long. Cut into 1" pieces.

3. Put sesame seeds into a deep bowl for easier coating.

4. Dip each piece of dough into the milk and then roll into sesame seeds. These should look like little logs, 1" x ¼". Place on non-stick cookie sheet and bake for 12 minutes. These cookies will continue to cook even after removing them from the oven. Makes 8 dozen.

Chocolate Almond Biscotti

(Time: 1 Hour)

Chocolate Almond Biscotti

NOTE: *These chocolate biscotti are wonderful with a cup of espresso or cappuccino and are great for dipping. The almond and the chocolate are meant for each other. Simply delicious!*

½ cup butter, softened
1¼ cups sugar
2 eggs
1 teaspoon almond extract

2¼ cups flour
¼ cup cocoa powder
1 teaspoon baking powder
¼ teaspoon salt
1 cup sliced almonds,
   or chopped coarse

1 cup semi sweet chocolate chips
1 tablespoon heavy cream

1. Preheat oven to 350°F. Combine butter and sugar in a large bowl. Beat with electric mixer until light and fluffy. Add eggs and almond extract and continue beating until light and lemon colored.

2. In another bowl, sift together flour, cocoa, baking powder, and salt. Blend into butter mixture until smooth. Stir in almonds. Divide dough in half and shape into 2 logs, about 10" long and 2" in diameter.

3. Place on lightly oiled baking sheet and bake for 25 to 30 minutes. Remove from oven and cool for about 15 minutes. Use a serrated knife and cut each log diagonally into ½" thick slices. Place slices back on baking sheet and bake about 3 minutes on each side.

4. Remove from oven and cool on wire rack. Melt chocolate chips and cream in microwave for about 1 minute, stirring until mixture is smooth. Drizzle the warm chocolate over each biscotti. Makes 36 biscotti.

Italian Fig Cookies

NOTE: *My mother, Ann Fiorino, would add these cookies to her Christmas cookie collection and hand out to friends for gifts. This recipe is very old and typically Italian.*

1½ cups dried figs
¾ cup light raisins
¼ cup slivered almonds

¼ cup granulated sugar
¼ cup hot water
¼ teaspoon ground cinnamon
dash of pepper

2½ cups all-purpose flour
⅓ cup granulated sugar
¼ teaspoon baking powder
½ cup shortening
2 tablespoons butter

½ cup milk
1 egg

Buttercream Frosting recipe
found on page 200

1. Preheat oven to 350°F. Put figs, raisins and almonds through food processor.

2. In mixing bowl, combine the sugar, water, cinnamon, and pepper. Stir into fruit mixture and set aside to be used for filling.

3. Combine flour, sugar, and baking powder. Cut the shortening and butter into the dry flour mixture until it resembles small peas. Beat the milk and egg together and stir into the dry mixture until moistened. Bring the dough together into a ball.

4. On lightly floured surface, roll dough into 18" x 16" rectangle. Cut into four 18" x 4" strips. Spread about ⅓ cup fig mixture onto the middle of each strip. Working with moistened hands, spread the filling from top of dough strip to bottom, using a little more if needed. Roll the strip of dough over the filling to make a log. Tuck the dough under and seal. Cut each into six 2½" lengths.

5. Place cookies seam-side down on ungreased cookie sheets. Curve each cookie slightly into a half-moon shape. Snip outer edge of curve three times with kitchen scissors.

6. Bake 20 to 25 minutes. Cool on rack, and frost with *Buttercream Frosting*.   Makes about 2½ dozen cookies.

Buttercream Frosting
(FOR ITALIAN FIG COOKIES)

NOTE: *This frosting stores well in the refrigerator and can be used for cakes as well as cookies.*

½ stick butter

4 cups powdered sugar

2 tablespoons milk

1 teaspoon almond or vanilla extract

1. Cream butter at room temperature with electric mixer. Gradually add sugar, beating until light and fluffy. Add milk and beat until spreading consistency. Stir in desired extract. Makes 3 cups.

Sicilian Slice Cookies

Sicilian Slice Cookies

NOTE: *These cookies are soft and warm when they first come out of the oven. They are wonderful eaten soon after or on the same day. However, they also make a tasty biscotti, if you desire.*

4 cups flour
4 teaspoons baking powder
6 eggs
1 tablespoon vanilla

1 cup vegetable shortening
1 cup granulated sugar
½ cup coarsely chopped pecans
½ cup chopped maraschino cherries, well drained
1 (12-ounce) package semi-sweet chocolate chips

confectioner's sugar

1. Preheat oven to 375°F. On waxed paper, sift together flour and baking powder three times. Set aside. Using electric mixer, beat eggs until slightly thick and lemon colored, 3 to 4 minutes. Stir in vanilla and set aside.

2. In large bowl, cream shortening with sugar until mixture is light and fluffy. Add beaten egg mixture to creamed mixture; blend together. Gradually add the creamed mixture to the dry ingredients, mixing well. Fold in pecans, cherries and chocolate chips.

3. Divide dough into thirds. Using moistened hands, form each third of dough into a long log, about 2" in diameter. Dough will be slightly sticky, but is easy to mold. Place logs on greased, floured cookie sheets, allowing room for logs to spread.

4. Bake for 20 to 25 minutes or until lightly browned. Remove logs from oven and cool about 20 minutes. When logs are just warm, cut into ½" slices, using a serrated knife with a sawing motion.

5. Cookies can be served at this time when dusted with confectioner's sugar or left on cookie sheet and toasted for about 3 minutes on each side to make biscottis.

6. Remove from oven and dust with confectioner's sugar. These cookies freeze or store well. Yields about 4 dozen.

(Time: 30 Minutes)

Anise Cookies

NOTE: *Anise cookies are an old Italian favorite. They are soft little cakes the first day and begin to get harder the next day. They are much enjoyed either way.*

4 cups all-purpose flour
1 cup sugar
6 tablespoons baking powder

2 larges eggs, beaten
½ cup whole milk
¾ cup olive oil
1 tablespoon anise extract

Anise Icing recipe found on page 205

1. Preheat oven to 375°F. In a large bowl, mix flour, sugar, and baking powder. Beat the eggs until frothy and lemon colored, and set aside. Make a well in the center of the flour mixture. Add the eggs, milk, oil, and anise. Mix together with flour until soft dough forms. If dough is too sticky or hard to handle, flour your hands. Using a teaspoon, take dough in hand and flatten to round shapes, about 1" around.

2. Place on lightly oiled baking sheet, 1" apart. Bake for 8 minutes. Top each cookie with Anise Icing while still warm. Makes about 4 dozen cookies.

Anise Icing

2 cups confectioner's sugar

2 teaspoons anise extract

2 tablespoons warm water

1. Combine all ingredients to make a thin icing. Dip the cookies in the icing while they are warm. Place on cookie sheet until the icing hardens, then remove to large platter. If more icing is needed, make up another batch. These cookies are best submerged in icing.

Sugared Pecan Balls

NOTE: *Some Italians make these cookies into large balls, about the size of quarters, but I like to make them a little smaller. These cookies will melt in your mouth. Better make another batch because they will be gone in no time.*

1 cup butter, room temperature

5 tablespoons granulated sugar

½ teaspoon salt

2 cups ground pecans

2 cups all-purpose flour

3 teaspoons vanilla

2 cups powdered sugar

1. Preheat oven to 325°F. Cream butter, sugar, and salt until smooth. Add the pecans, flour, and vanilla; using your hands to mix thoroughly. Form dough into small balls and place on un-greased cookie sheet. Bake in preheated oven for 15 to 20 minutes. Watch cookies closely; they are done when brown on bottom.

2. Roll the cookies while still warm in powdered sugar, being careful not to break. Place on cook-ie platter and sift additional powdered sugar over cookies. To make colorful during Christmas, add a few drops red or green food coloring to dough. Makes about 6 dozen cookies, depend-ing on how small or large the balls are made.

(Time: 15 Minutes)

Zabaglione with Berries
(ITALIAN CUSTARD)

NOTE: *Zabaglione custard is an old popular Italian dessert and can be found in some authentic Italian restaurants. The custard is fragile and doesn't last for a long time. It is best eaten soon after making.*

8 egg yolks
¾ cup sugar
1 teaspoon vanilla extract
1 teaspoon brandy extract

1 cup frozen blackberries and raspberries mixed, or berry medley
sugar

1. In metal bowl, beat the egg yolks about 3 minutes. Transfer bowl over a heavy pot filled with about 2" water. Water should not be boiling or touching bowl. Over low heat beat the egg yolks an additional 7 minutes. Mixture should be thick and smooth. Remove from heat and continue beating if not thick enough. Fold in the vanilla and brandy extract.

2. Divide the custard between 4 long stemmed glasses or 6 custard cups, depending on desired servings and top with berries sprinkled with sugar. Serve warm immediately or place custard cups in refrigerator until time of serving. Serves 4 or 6.

Bocconcini con Crema
(ITALIAN CRÉME PUFFS)

NOTE: *These light cream puffs literally melt in your mouth, and can be whipped up within an hour. Serve warm with custard or cool with other cream fillings. Double for a large crowd. Sprinkle top with powdered sugar.*

2 cups water

1 cup butter (2 sticks)

½ teaspoon salt

2 cups sifted flour

8 eggs

1. Preheat oven to 400°F. In a medium saucepan, combine water, butter, and salt. Bring to a boil and remove from heat. Add flour all at once and stir with slotted spoon until flour comes together in a ball. Add the eggs one at a time, beating well after each egg to a smooth satin consistency. Drop by 2 heaping tablespoons, 2" apart, on large ungreased baking sheet. Go back to each dollop of dough and add 1 tablespoon on top for a "cap." There should be enough dough for 15 cream puffs.

2. Bake in oven for 40 to 45 minutes. Puffs should be well browned and hollow feeling. Cool, and with sharp knife, cut off "cap" crosswise. Remove any surface "wet" dough and keep the rest intact. Fill with the filling of your choice; see **Custard Pudding** recipe found on page 209, **Mascarpone Cream Filling** recipe found on page 210, or **Cream Cheese and Ricotta Filling** recipe found on page 212. All are very delicious and can be used as variations for different occasions. Makes 15 puffs.

Custard Pudding
(FOR ITALIAN CRÉME PUFFS)

NOTE: *This is a rich custard pudding, one of my families favorites. I have used it for years when catering Italian dinners to community functions.*

⅔ cup sugar
½ teaspoon salt
2½ tablespoons cornstarch
1 tablespoon flour
2¾ cups whole milk

3 egg yolks, beaten fluffy
1 tablespoon vanilla
1 tablespoon butter

1. Mix sugar, salt, cornstarch, and flour in 3-quart saucepan. Stir in milk slowly and cook over medium heat stirring constantly, using a slotted plastic spoon or spatula. Cook until mixture thickens and begins to boil. Boil gently for 1 minute, scraping bottom of pan to avoid burning. Remove from heat. Slowly pour half of mixture into beaten egg yolks, stirring constantly with a whisk, then blend egg yolk mixture into remaining hot pudding in saucepan. Boil gently 1 more minute. Add the vanilla and butter.

2. Turn off heat. Continue to cook until butter melts and custard is thick. Cool; fill cream puffs. This recipe needs to be doubled to fill 15 baked puffs. Sift powdered sugar over each cream puff.

Mascarpone Cream Filling
(FOR ITALIAN CRÉME PUFFS)

NOTE: *This is another variation of Italian crème puff filling. The filling is so light and creamy, and it is wonderful with just the powdered sugar or served with a glaze or sauce.*

2 (8-ounce) cartons mascarpone Italian cream cheese

2 cups heavy whipping cream

⅔ cup sugar, or more for your taste

1 tablespoon vanilla

powdered sugar

or **Chocolate Glaze** recipe found on page 211

1. Spoon mascarpone cheese into a large bowl. Set aside. Beat heavy cream with sugar using electric beater until stiff, but not butter consistency. Add the vanilla and mascarpone cheese to the whipped cream mixture and continue to beat until smooth and satiny. Cut "caps" off tops of cooled baked puffs. Remove any surface "wet" dough and leave the rest intact.

2. Fill with cream mixture. Return the "caps" on top, letting some of the cream show through.

3. Sprinkle with powdered sugar or use the Chocolate Glaze recipe over top. Makes enough cream filling for 10 to 12 puffs.

Chocolate Glaze

NOTE: *Use over cream puffs with **Mascarpone Cream Filling** recipe found on page 210.*

1 cup semisweet chocolate chips

2 tablespoons unsalted butter

2 tablespoons light corn syrup

3 tablespoons cream

1. Over very low heat in heavy small pot, melt the chocolate chips and butter, stirring constantly. Remove from heat. Add the corn syrup and cream. Return to heat and stir together until blended. Makes 1 cup glaze.

(Time: 15 Minutes)

Cream Cheese & Ricotta
(FILLING FOR ITALIAN CRÈME PUFFS)

NOTE: *This ricotta filling is very similar to that of cannoli filling, but has a heavier consistency by using the mascarpone cheese. It is very rich, smooth, and addicting. Serve these cool, with lots of powdered sugar sprinkled on top.*

2 cups heavy whipping cream

2 (8-ounce) cartons mascarpone Italian cheese

⅔ cup sugar, or more for your taste

1 cup ricotta cheese

1 teaspoon vanilla extract

⅓ cup drained chopped maraschino cherries

1. Pour cream into large bowl. Using electric beater, beat until stiff, but not butter consistency. Add the mascarpone cheese and sugar. Beat together until smooth and satiny. Fold in the ricotta, vanilla, and cherries. Filling should be thick and smooth. Test for taste, adding a little more sugar if desired.

2. Cut "caps" off tops of cooled baked puffs. Remove any surface "wet" dough and leave the rest intact.

3. Fill with cream cheese mixture. Return "caps" to puffs; sprinkle with powdered sugar. Makes enough filling for 12 to 15 puffs.

Italian Cannoli Shells

(Time: 1 Hour and 15 Minutes)

$\mathcal{H}$omemade Italian Cannoli Shells

NOTE: *These shells are golden and crisp. Fill them with the ricotta filling sprinkled with the pow-dered sugar and you have a classic Italian dessert. Cannoli shell forms can be purchased at specialty kitchen stores. Don't be afraid to tackle these. Once you have made them, you'll feel confident to make them again and again.*

1¼ cups flour, divided
¼ teaspoon salt
1 tablespoon sugar

2 tablespoons soft unsalted butter
1 large egg, beaten
2 tablespoons milk

metal cannoli tube forms, 5" long
1 egg white, beaten
4 cups olive oil for deep-frying cannoli shells

1. Place 1 cup flour in a mound on clean counter. Add salt and sugar and mix together. Work in the softened butter until the flour becomes "mealy." Make a well in the middle of the flour and add the beaten egg and the milk. Work the flour into the egg mixture and bring the dough together, adding the remaining ¼ cup flour. The dough should be soft and pliable. On floured board, roll the dough out, turning often and sprinkling with added flour to keep the dough from sticking. Roll the dough to a square about 12" by 12". The dough should be very thin, about the thickness of a rolled noodle. Cut squares 3" by 3". This recipe should yield about 16 cannoli squares.

2. Place cannoli form diagonally on each dough square. Wrap pastry around form, one corner over the other. Seal corners with egg white.

3. In 3-quart pot, heat oil to 375°F. Deep-fry 3 shells at a time. Using a fork inserted into one end of the form, turn the shells once to brown evenly. These shells cook quickly, in about 1½ min-utes. Using a fork tine, remove from pot when they are golden brown and crisp.

4. Lay hot shells on paper towels to drain and let cool about 3 minutes. Gently hold forms with paper towel and push cooked shells off form (they will not break). Continue to wrap forms with dough and deep fry, until all the squares have been used. When completely cooled fill each shell with **Cannoli Filling** recipe found on page 215. Dust with powdered sugar and serve. Makes 16 cannoli-filled shells.

(Time: 20 Minutes)

Cannoli Filling
(FOR ITALIAN CANNOLIS)

NOTE: *Cannoli pastry shells are best hand-made, but if short on time, purchase ready-made. Shells can be found in Italian stores or in some large grocery chains. Look for them in the bakery department. Make the filling ahead and refrigerate. This is a classic Italian dessert. It is one that you will definitely want to serve, especially with a good cup of espresso.*

15 homemade or ready-to-serve cannoli shells

1 cup heavy whipping cream
3 tablespoons sugar
1½ teaspoons vanilla

2 cups ricotta cheese
2 tablespoons maraschino cherries, drained, and chopped fine
2 tablespoons small chocolate chips

½ cup chopped pecan pieces, more if needed
maraschino cherries, halved, for garnishing ends of cannolis

1. With an electric beater, whip the cream, adding the sugar a little at a time. Add the vanilla, and beat until stiff peaks form. Add the ricotta, 2 tablespoons cherries, and 2 tablespoons chocolate chips. Fold gently together.

2. Using a small spoon or spatula, fill cannoli shell first from one end and then the other. Press filling gently to make sure centers are full. Scrape ends to smooth cream. Dip ends in chopped pecans and garnish with a maraschino cherry. Arrange filled cannoli shells on large platter. Sift powdered sugar over all. Makes 15 filled shells.

Sfingi

(Time: 3 Hours to rise and 15 Minutes to fry)

Sfingi
(ITALIAN PUFF PASTRY)

NOTE: *This recipe comes from my sister-in-law, Rose Marie Fiorino, who has made these wonderful pastries for many years at all of our special gatherings. In Italian we call them "sfingis", meaning "puffs."*

2 cups flour
¼ teaspoon salt
1 teaspoon sugar

6 eggs, beaten
½ cup warm water
1 teaspoon yeast

3 cups olive oil for deep frying
1 cup sugar to sprinkle puffs
  or ½ cup honey with ½ cup pecans, chopped fine

1. In large bowl mix the flour, salt, and sugar together. Make a "well" in center of flour. Beat the eggs until fluffy and light; set aside. Add the yeast to the warm water and let stand about 8 minutes, until the yeast begins to foam up. Pour the yeast water in the "well," and add the eggs. Using a large whisk, mix the flour, water, and egg mixture a little at a time until well blended. This dough will be very soupy.

2. Cover with plastic wrap and let sit for 3 hours. The dough will rise to the top of the bowl and "bubble".

3. In a large deep saucepan, heat about 3 cups olive oil or more for frying. Drop a teaspoon of dough into the oil. If it "puffs up" the oil is hot enough. Drop by teaspoons into the hot oil. The dough will puff up nicely and brown evenly. Turn the pastry once to brown the same on both sides, about 2 to 3 minutes total. Cook about 6 or more at a time, depending on how large the saucepan is. Remove with slotted spoon onto paper towel.

4. Sprinkle heavily with sugar while hot or dip sides of puffs in honey, then in chopped pecans. Either way is very good. Keep frying the "puffs" until all the dough is used. These are best eaten warm. Makes about 4 dozen.

Pineapple Upside-down Cake

NOTE: *While this cake is not Italian, I have used it on my catering list for as long as I can remember. It is the ever-popular cake and I promised my friends I would include it. Don't be afraid to use olive oil. It is the only oil I ever use.*

1 Pillsbury Moist Supreme yellow cake mix

1 cup water

⅓ cup mild olive oil

3 eggs

½ cup butter

2 cups light brown sugar

1 (20-ounce) can pineapple slices, or chunks, drained

8 to 10 maraschino cherries

Sugar Glazed Pecans recipe found on page 223, optional

1. Preheat oven to 350°F. In large bowl, mix by hand the cake mix, water, oil, and eggs, just until all lumps are dissolved. Do not over-mix.

2. In a 13" x 9" baking pan add the melted butter, coating the bottom of the pan evenly. Add the brown sugar and spread evenly over the butter. Arrange the drained pineapple slices or chunks over the brown sugar. Place a maraschino cherry in the center of each pineapple ring. If using chunks, cut some of the big chunks in half and place the cherries in various places around the chunks. If using the glazed pecans, place them around the pineapples. Now add the cake batter over all.

3. Bake in preheated oven for 35 minutes or until middle of cake springs back. Remove cake from oven. Loosen sides of cake with a spatula. Place a large cookie sheet over the cake and using both hands and pot-holders, flip the cake over all at once onto the cookie sheet. Be sure to hold the cookie sheet over the cake pan while flipping. Cake should flip out nicely. Serve warm or at room temperature. Makes 12 large slices.

Tiramisù

NOTE: *I did not grow up with Tiramisù. It was not popular until the early 1990's. However, it is now one of the most popular of Italian desserts. Tiramisù means "pick-me-up". The whipped cream topping is optional, but does add a nice final touch if you prefer.*

2½ to 3 cups strong cooled espresso coffee
⅓ cup sugar
48 Italian ladyfinger cookies

2 small Hershey chocolate candy bars,
   chopped or grated
unsweetened cocoa for dusting

8 egg yolks
¾ cup sugar

1 cup heavy cream
¼ cup sugar
1 teaspoon brandy extract

2 cups heavy cream
⅓ cup sugar
2 teaspoons brandy extract
2 (8-ounce) cartons mascarpone cheese

chocolate swirls to garnish

1. Make the espresso coffee and add the ⅓ cup sugar. Let dissolve together and let stand until cooled. One at a time, dip 24 ladyfingers in the espresso, and place on bottom of a 12" x 9" baking dish. You will have three rows of 8 ladyfingers on the first layer. Cradle the soaked ladyfingers in your hand to avoid breaking as you place them.

2. Next, beat the egg yolks in a large glass bowl, adding the ¾ cup sugar a little at a time for 10 minutes. The eggs will form a thick, smooth custard. Set aside. Beat the cream with the sugar until stiff peaks form. Add the brandy extract and the two cartons of mascarpone cheese to the whipped cream. Using mixer, beat the mascarpone cheese and whipped cream mixture together, just until smooth. Fold the cream/cheese mixture into the egg custard until all are incorporated and smooth. Pour one-half of the mixture over the first soaked ladyfingers. Sprinkle one of the chopped candy bars over the top, and using a sifter, dust the chocolate with unsweetened cocoa.

3. Dip the remaining 24 ladyfingers in the coffee and repeat the same process of layering, until all the ladyfingers and cream/cheese mixture are used. Spread the remaining chopped chocolate bar over the second layer and dust with sifted cocoa.

4. Beat the remaining cream and sugar until stiff peaks form. Fold in the brandy extract. Spread over the Tiramisù and garnish the top with the chocolate swirls and dust with unsweetened cocoa. Cover with plastic wrap and refrigerate 4 to 6 hours or overnight until all the flavors have settled and the cake is firm. Serves 12.

Rosalie's *Italian Cream Cake*

(Time: 1 Hour)

Rosalie's Italian Cream Cake

NOTE: *This cake is not only scrumptious, but stands tall and elegant on your cake stand. It has been the rave among my Italian desserts. Frost with cream cheese frosting.*

1 cup buttermilk
1 teaspoon baking soda

½ cup butter
2 cups sugar
½ cup mild olive oil
5 egg yolks

2 cups all purpose flour
1½ teaspoon vanilla

5 egg whites
1 cup shredded coconut
1 cup chopped pecan pieces
unsalted butter

Cream Cheese Frosting recipe
found on page 222
Sugar Glazed Pecans recipe
found on page 223
Toasted Coconut recipe
found on page 224
3 large maraschino or bing cherries

1. Preheat oven to 325 degrees. Combine buttermilk and baking soda in a two-cup measure to allow room for mixture to foam up. Set aside. Beat butter and sugar until creamy. Add olive oil slowly until blended. Continue to beat until mixture is smooth and shiny. Add egg yolks one at a time and beat well after each addition. Add buttermilk mixture and flour, alternately a little at a time, until both are used. Stir in vanilla.

2. Clean beaters and beat egg whites until stiff. Fold egg whites gently into batter. Stir in coconut and pecans. Pour into three 9" cake pans, greased with unsalted butter and dusted with flour. Bake at 325 degrees for 30 to 32 minutes. Cool cakes on racks.

3. Frost with Cream Cheese Frosting; garnish with Sugar Glazed Pecans and Toasted Coconut.

4. To assemble cake: begin with first layer, putting round-side down on cake stand; frost with cream cheese icing. Continue with layers ending with round-side up. Frost the top and sides of cake liberally with icing. Place the cherries in center of the cake. Place the coconut around cherries up to about 3" out and around cherries. Place sugared pecans all around edge of cake. Makes sixteen ½" slices.

Cream Cheese Frosting

NOTE: *Cool frosting in refrigerator about 30 minutes before frosting cake. This recipe makes enough to frost the **Rosalie's Italian Cream Cake** recipe found on page 221. You will have plenty to spare between layers as well as for sides and top. If you should have some left over, use for topping on French toast, bagels, and fruit.*

1 stick butter
2 (8-ounce) packages Philadelphia Cream Cheese, softened
4 cups powdered sugar
2 teaspoons vanilla

1. Whip butter and cream cheese together with electric mixer until blended. Mixing ½ stick of butter and 1 package of cheese at a time is much easier. Then combine in one bowl. Add powdered sugar 1 cup at a time, blending well with creamed mixture. Add vanilla at the end and continue to whip together. Makes about 4 cups frosting.

(Time: 5 Minutes)

Sugar Glazed Pecans

NOTE: *This recipe can easily be doubled and used to garnish ice cream or cakes or is just good for snacks.*

⅓ cup whole pecans
1 to 2 teaspoons sugar
1 small skillet

1. Put pecans in skillet and sprinkle with the sugar. Turn heat to medium and begin stirring pecans. Sugar will begin to melt. Continue stirring until a glaze forms on pecans and they become slightly browned. Remove from heat and place on waxed paper to cool. Use for garnish on **Rosalie's Italian Cream Cake** recipe found on page 221 and the **Nutella Pancakes and Sugar Glazed Pecans** recipe found on page 38.

Toasted Coconut

NOTE: *Toasting the coconut adds a crunchy sweetness that really enhances your dessert. Use this on pies and cakes.*

⅓ cup shredded coconut
1 small skillet

1. Put coconut in small skillet. Turn heat to medium. Stir coconut constantly until coconut begins to turn golden brown. Coconut can burn quickly. Remove from heat and continue to stir a few more times. Pour coconut onto waxed paper and cool. Garnish for **Rosalie's Italian Cream Cake** recipe found on page 221.

$Strawberries$ $\&$ $Cream$ $Cake$

NOTE: *Italians use a yellow sponge cake for this recipe, but I have found that a yellow box cake has a better taste. Filling the layers with strawberries and cream cheese gives the cake an elegant appearance.*

1 yellow cake mix
unsalted butter

1 (8 ounce) carton mascarpone
  or Philadelphia cream cheese
1 cup powdered sugar
1 cup heavy whipping cream
1 teaspoon vanilla

1 quart fresh strawberries
¼ cup sugar

powdered sugar for garnish

1. Preheat oven to 350°F. Prepare cake mix according to package directions, using light olive oil instead of vegetable oil. Pour mixture into two 9" greased cake pans, using unsalted butter, and dusted with flour. Bake 30 minutes. Remove to cake rack and cool.

2. With electric mixture, beat the cheese and powdered sugar together until creamy. Add the whipping cream and vanilla and continue to beat together until mixture becomes smooth. Refrigerate 30 minutes before using.

3. Wash and drain the strawberries. Cut off steams and slice thin. Add the sugar and toss together. Set aside.

4. With a long serrated knife, cut the cake layers in half, making four layers. On a large cake platter, place one layer cut-side up. Spoon a dollop of cream cheese on the layer and spread evenly. Spread ¼ of the strawberries over the cheese. Continue spreading the cheese/strawberry mixture on each layer. Top the last layer round-side down. Use remainder of cheese and strawberries on top. Sift powdered sugar on top and side of cake. Refrigerate cake until set. Serves 8.

Lemon
Ice

(Time: 10 Minutes)

Italian Lemon Ice

NOTE: *Lemon ice is an Italian tradition and a light touch after a large meal. For a large picnic crowd, use a 5-gallon container and increase the ingredients accordingly.*

1 gallon crushed ice
1 large can frozen lemonade
juice of 1 lemon
1 cup sugar, more or less to taste, depending
   on how sweet or tart desired
maraschino cherries

1. Mix all ingredients together and serve in clear party cups or glasses. Garnish each glass with 1 maraschino cherry. Cups of lemon ice can be made ahead and kept in freezer until ready to serve. Makes about 32 half-cup servings.

$\mathcal{S}$heraton's Famous Cheesecake

NOTE: *Rumor has it that this cheesecake was once on the menu at the exclusive Sheraton Hotel in St. Louis Missouri. I received it from a dear friend years ago and always reserved it for my special catering occasions. It is worthy to be served at a "black-tie special" and is truly a "mouthful of bliss". Serve it with a light Italian dish such as **Italian Crusted Chicken** found on page 184 and vegetable of your choice.*

1 - 10" spring-form pan
  or 1 - 10" tin pie pan, deep

½ cup melted butter
¼ cup sugar
2 cups graham cracker crumbs

4 (8 ounce) packages of cream cheese
4 eggs
1 cup plus 2 tablespoons sugar
1 teaspoon vanilla

1 (8 ounce) carton sour cream
¼ cup sugar
1 teaspoon lemon juice

Pineapple Sauce recipe found on page 229, optional

1. Preheat oven to 325°F. Combine butter, sugar, and graham cracker crumbs. Press into the bottom and up the sides of the ungreased pan. Set aside.

2. In large mixing bowl beat cream cheese with electric mixer until smooth. Add eggs, sugar, and vanilla. Continue beating until blended well to a satin-like mixture. Pour filling over crust. Bake 1 hour and 10 minutes or until set in the middle. Cheese cake will form cracks on top, which is expected. Remove from oven and let cool completely.

3. Combine sour cream, sugar, and lemon juice. Spread evenly over top of cake. Chill at least four hours before serving. Serve plain or with Pineapple Sauce Recipe. Makes 16 servings.

Pineapple Sauce

NOTE: *This a great sauce to spoon over **Sheraton's Famous Cheesecake** found on page 228. It is also great on coffee cakes, crepes, and pancakes.*

1 (20 ounce) can crushed pineapples, undrained

3 tablespoons corn starch

2 tablespoons butter

⅓ cup sugar

½ teaspoon vanilla

1. Mix pineapples, corn starch, sugar and vanilla in a bowl until corm starch and sugar have dissolved. Pour into saucepan and over medium heat, bring mixture to gentle boil. Add butter. Lower heat while stirring constantly until mixture thickens. Remove from heat and bring to room temperature. Serve over your favorite dessert.

ROSALIE AND "CAPPUCCINO"

230 Rosalie Serving Italian

ROSALIE SERVING
SCOTT AND JENNIFER HARPOLE

GRANDMA AND GRANDPA FIORINO

GRANDMA AND GRANDPA CASTROGIOVANNI

"Live well,
Love much,
and
Laugh often."

ELIJAH HARPOLE SCHULTZ

INDEX:

INDEX:

General Index:

General Index:

General Index: